PRACTICAL MANPOWER PLANNING

John Bramham was born in 1944. He
graduated from Manchester University
in 1966 with a degree in Psychology
and then studied Personnel
Management at Leeds Polytechnic.

He joined North Eastern Gas in Leeds
and after training worked in industrial
relations and other areas of personnel
work. In 1973 he moved to the
headquarters of British Gas as
Manpower Planning Manager. He is
currently Industrial Relations Manager
in the Northern Region of British Gas
plc in Newcastle-upon-Tyne.

He is married and has two young
daughters. His chief hobbies are
gardening, making films, teaching,
chess, education and visiting the
countryside.

To Helen and Wendy

who should remember that . . .

*"With so much at stake
On decisions they make
It has entered their corporate noddles
That the learned professors
Might lessen the stresses
By recourse to computerised models*

*But decisions my friend
Are a means not an end
And its 'how' more than 'what' that may matter,
So the wise are as ever
More use than the clever–
Since there's more decisions than data."*

from a poem by Bertie Rambsbottom
reproduced with kind permission

Practical Manpower Planning

Fourth edition

JOHN BRAMHAM

Institute of Personnel Management

First published 1975
Second edition 1978
Third edition 1982
Fourth edition 1988
Reprinted 1989, 1990 *and* 1992

© Institute of Personnel Management,
1975, 1978, 1982, 1988

British Library Cataloguing in Publication Data

    Bramham, John
    Practical manpower planning.—4th ed.
    1. Manpower planning.   Management aspects
    I. Title
    658.3'01

ISBN 0-85292-404-6

Printed in Great Britain by Martin's of Berwick Ltd, Berwick upon Tweed

Contents

Acknowledgements

My greatest debt is to C L Davies, erstwhile Personnel Director of North Eastern Gas, and his deputy, G G Bennett, who gave me the opportunity and the resources to develop an understanding of some of the modern methods of manpower management described in this book.

In addition it is impossible for me to say how much my ideas owe to the help and advice given to me over a number of years by C Purkiss, B Morris and A R Smith and many other friends and colleagues in the IPM, the Manpower Society and elsewhere. I am grateful for the help and guidance of my colleagues in British Gas, especially C M I Clough who has helped me understand many of the quantitative aspects of manpower planning. I should like to thank G G Bennet, A R Smith, N M Johnston and N J Urwin who read the manuscript and made many helpful comments. The book is better as a result of their efforts.

My thanks are due to Anne Staddon and Maureen Melvin who prepared much of the typescript, and especially to my wife Susan for all her help and tolerance.

Finally what is written is my own responsibility and the opinions expressed are not necessarily shared by my employer, British Gas.

John T Bramham
vii

Preface

I have tried to write an easily readable book for practising personnel managers and officers who are starting in manpower planning or who wish to know something more about it. It should also be of value to the line manager. This is a general guide with simple practical ideas. The manager who wishes to study more widely, or in greater depth, will find the references useful.

The book deals with what has been variously called organization, enterprise or company manpower planning. Consequently it will not satisfy the reader who is interested in national manpower planning for its own sake. This is only mentioned here when it is of direct concern to the manager.

It is worth remembering that each author can draw only on his own experience and reading. Consequently, while I have tried to generalize from my experience and to bring out principles applicable in many situations, it is inevitable that another author or manager would consider a different emphasis to be more appropriate.

While it is intended that the book should stand as a whole, many people may wish to skip the more detailed chapters and will gain a general appreciation of the background problems and framework of manpower planning in chapters 1 and 2 without reading further.

Chapters 3 - 9 deal with specific aspects of manpower planning. Chapter 3 considers how to identify requirements and, while not using statistical techniques, recognizes their importance when properly used. Chapters 4 and 5 deal with manpower supply analysis and forecasting. Chapter 4 looks at age, promotions and so on, while chapter 5 deals exclusively with wastage analysis and forecasting. Chapter 6 looks at some problems in formulating manpower plans and emphasizes the need for flexibility and a continuous planning process, with limited faith placed in the 'plan'.

Chapter 7 looks at manpower control reporting and costs. This area is important if plans are to be achieved and if the commercial criteria by which many organizations are primarily judged are to be satisfied. Chapter 8 considers information, stressing that information is needed for decision making. In deciding information needs the manager first asks which decisions he wishes to affect. Chapter 9 deals with computers and models in manpower planning. This is a subject which simultaneously excites approval and anguish from supporters and detractors. It has become one of the hallmarks of manpower planning. It is not of course their use but their misuse that leads to difficulties.

The final chapter sets out some speculative areas for future development and suggests ways in which progress can be made.

London 1975

Preface to third edition

In preparing this third edition of *Practical Manpower Planning* I have taken the opportunity to make corrections and to update where required. The main change, however, has been the complete revision of the first chapter. The techniques and tools available in manpower planning have not changed substantially since the mid 1970s, though the use of the computer is more obvious and the climate of manpower management has changed dramatically.

This third edition suggests that there is less need to place emphasis on mechanisms and technicalities, which for some became an obsession, and that we should recognize that successful planning arises when questions are asked and problems approached correctly, rather than in always seeking the 'right forecast'.

I am grateful to the many readers who have taken the trouble to write and contact me with comments and questions on previous editions. Where appropriate I have revised accordingly. I am particularly grateful for the continuing support of colleagues in the manpower field which remains invaluable.

March 1982

Preface to fourth edition

This fourth edition is written at a time when there is a prospect of real growth and creativity in our approach to people at work. The first edition, written in 1974/75, expressed a hope that open management and treating employees fairly and with integrity might create the partnership in organizations that would lead to adaptability and a ready acceptance of change. The 1980s have shown some promise that this is being recognized. Problems in planning and true strategic thinking are not to be solved by ever more specific refinements to our planning tools, though tools and techniques remain important.

Throughout much of the industrial world the task is centred on equality, flexibility, change, adaptability — these are good words for manpower planning. Therefore, while the techniques may be similar, the motivational thinking that is framing modern personnel practice in companies gives some grounds for optimism.

John T Bramham
March 1988

1 Manpower planning and flexibility

To facilitate the management of materials, money and people a range of management disciplines have emerged. These include market planning, production management, financial control, business administration, human resource management and so on.

Of these, human resource management (or what one might normally prefer to call personnel management) is the least disciplined of disciplines; a market place for every pedlar of far fetched ideas; an amalgam of theory and practice, personalized fantasy, shrewd application of experience, dull dogma, soaring flights of the imagination and sheer drivel.

Personnel specialists have spawned a profession with a disposition for new words and pseudo quantification. The language of hard bitten trade union negotiators lives side by side, if uneasily, with terminology such as 'role overload' (which means busy), 'cohort analysis' (which means group leavers rate), 'organization development' (which refers to managing change) or 'negative recruitment' (which means redundancy), 'personnel turbulence' (instead of high leaving rates), 'multi-functional-diagonal-sliced, cluster group' (for a working party) and one sociologist's description of a strike as a 'negative response to the work situation'.

While manpower planning practitioners are not free from intellectual self-indulgence in this matter, discipline, order, fact and information increasingly influence personnel decision-making. Manpower planning is not so much another personnel discipline as an approach to personnel management which aims to add a further dimension to the management of people at work.

FIGURE 1
Flexibility

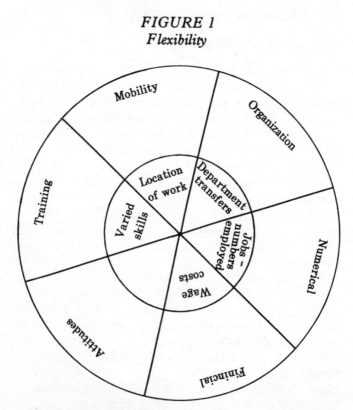

Surveys have shown that personnel people spent a great deal of their time on operational matters. They recruited today the employees they needed today and trained today the people who needed training today; little or no thought was given to tomorrow's needs (indeed management knew so little about personnel requirements that in fact it recruited and trained what was needed yesterday because management could not determine what today's requirements were, let alone tomorrow's). This point has been emphasized by P F Drucker who criticized personnel professionals for being firefighters with little or no concern for the future development and problems of the organization.

FIGURE 2

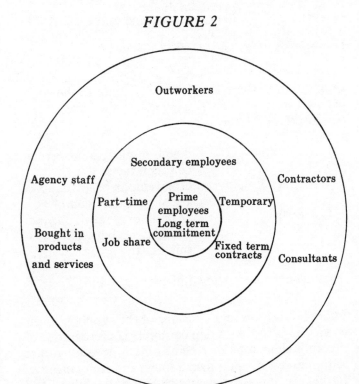

The flexible firm

After the words 'manpower' and 'personnel' and their derivatives, 'flexibility' and its derivatives is the most commonly used concept in this text. No 'plan' or 'blueprint' will be relevant for long — the pace of change experienced in the organization requires adaptability and creativity — in short, a flexible approach to planning (see references at end of text).

What form does this flexibility take? There are 6 main areas in which flexibility can be sought:

TRAINING	— SKILLS FLEXIBILITY
MOBILITY	— LOCATION FLEXIBILITY
ORGANIZATION	— DEPARTMENT FLEXIBILITY
NUMERICAL	— JOB FLEXIBILITY
FINANCIAL	— WAGE-COST FLEXIBILITY
ATTITUDE	— EMPLOYEES' VIEW OF FLEXIBILITY

In addition to these areas they can apply to the company's 'workers' (not 'employees' as they are not all employed) at 3 levels:

Prime Employees:	direct employees on permanent contracts
Secondary Employees:	direct employees on temporary or part-time contracts
Outworkers:	not employees at all but contractors, agency staff, consultants and so on.

These concepts are shown in Figures 1 and 2.

These levels represent divisions of the supply of manpower. This concentration on supply is a recognition of the unlikelihood of ever being able to forecast future requirements in other than a rough and ready manner. In the face of inaccurate assessments of the future, and the need to adapt to any change that might occur, the solution is internal flexibility. This can be flexibility of PRIME employees, who can do a wide range of jobs over a variety of working hours, or it can involve bringing in new SECONDARY or OUTWORKERS on contracts who can be dispensed with as soon as required.

This type of flexibility is the strategic answer to the difficulties experienced by managers who have lost the ability to hire and fire at will. Of course, the demands on prime employees are likely to be high, as they will undertake a variety of jobs at a variety of locations and learn new skills as required. It therefore follows that their personal commitment is crucial. The most important prerequisite for flexibility is therefore a flexible attitude on the part of the employee. This need for personal commitment in turn requires the organization to focus on the employee as a key asset not as a cost. This emergence of the employee as the centre and focus of creativity and change is long overdue. It is the theme that underlies modern approaches to personnel management which have become known as 'Human Resource Management'.

This concept of manpower planning has made an impact on personnel managers. Although the personnel professional has to be good at firefighting, gradually planning and development and flexible approaches to management are affecting the way the job is done.

While the manager can look to manpower planning to improve the management of personnel matters it is important to stress that it is not a lifeline that can be thrown to a company in distress. In order to clarify the nature of the contribution of manpower planning it may be helpful to liken it to the practice of navigation:

The good navigator uses scientific methods in applying his knowledge and skills, within the limits of the equipment available, in order to establish first his

5

position and then his best possible course and speed, with a view to arriving at a chosen destination by the most suitable route. From time to time during the voyage he will take fresh readings; calculate what action is necessary to compensate for hitherto unforeseen changes in wind, current and weather; and adjust his course accordingly. If the wind changes dramatically the navigator is not likely to abandon compass and sextant, go below and pray to the gods to get him to port. He is more likely to apply his knowledge and skills to a reassessment of his position and course as soon as this is practicable.

(A R Smith, reference 7b)

If the manager is only concerned with a trip around the boating lake, sophisticated methods of navigation are not required; but if you want to round Cape Horn in winter, good planning is essential.

The same maxims hold true when managing human resources. In a small family business the manager might survive without planning; but most managers are concerned with organizations of extreme complexity that operate in extremes of difficulty, struggling for survival and growth. In this environment, planning, rigorous analysis and control are the best tools that the manager has to ensure that events are controlled rather than have events determine company activities.

Is planning a fruitless activity?

It has often been argued that planning and forecasting is so difficult it is hardly worth the effort. It may be easier to take a compass reading on a local lake than in a force 10 gale, but a reading on a boating lake is of little value, while a reading in a gale may be vital for survival.

Even the best laid plans go awry. A navigator may have to replot the route several times during a voyage but he does not assume that navigation is NOT worthwhile, but rather the opposite. It may be necessary, in the face of unforeseen problems, to change route and reassess prospects but, by using specialized equipment and techniques, you are more likely to arrive at a chosen destination than by simply drifting with the wind and currents.

It is of course a paradox that as it becomes more difficult to predict and select, so it becomes more necessary to do so. The 19th century businessman would have found his 20th century counterpart's obsession with planning strange. But, of course, the environment is now changing more rapidly and the conflicting pressures are greater. The modern manager must develop systems and controls which increase the likelihood of the environment being controlled to a reasonable extent. Without an accurate awareness of his position, a manager will quickly lose his way in this rapidly changing environment.

Criticisms of forecasting and planning often imply that there is a choice between undertaking manpower planning and not doing so. In practice the real choice is whether to be systematic in planning or to be swept along by events. Decisions are made whether or not they are planned, but even rudimentary planning will improve the quality of the decisions made.

If something unforeseen occurs the manager's knowledge of the environment should enable him to adapt. Manpower planning is concerned with preserving flexibility in uncertain situations; with developing policies and making decisions today which will affect the workforce tomorrow.

Emergence of manpower planning

Manpower planning emerged as the cost of employment rose, both in terms of training and wage costs. In certain circumstances, when pressures created by the

7

workforce combine with external forces, costs can rise very rapidly. These forces manifested themselves in a variety of ways, often directly in the form of shortages, surpluses or costs of people. These frequently emerged because of technological change in the office or on the factory floor. Underlining this was a quickening pace of social and political change, exacerbated by resource and energy problems. Internally the company has often found itself faced with worsening industrial relations brought about because managers failed to persuade employees to accept the changes that relatively poor economic performance and declining competitiveness made necessary.

Economic performance

In the first edition of *Practical Manpower Planning* it was considered necessary to demonstrate poor UK performance in graphs and charts. It is interesting to note that although people currently argue about the solutions, causes and extent of our problems, there would be few today who would deny that companies which are largely characterized by overmanning and low wages, under-utilization of capital and labour, low capital investment, low profits and poor industrial relations will fail. This text will argue that the personnel manager, particularly through his relationship with trade unions, is well placed with his line management colleagues to identify and correct poor performance and the under-employment of people and machines within the company.

The essential features of manpower planning

Manpower planning practice can be separated into three general areas of activity

    (i)   macro manpower planning
    (ii) company (or micro) manpower planning
    (iii) techniques of manpower planning

8

Macro manpower planning is carried out at a national level. This includes the overall management of the economy in respect of employment and education and frequently involves political issues. This text deals only briefly with these matters as far as they affect, and can be influenced by, companies. The belief that the government, by detailed national planning, can do more than create the *framework* within which organizations operate is doomed to be unfulfilled (see Supplementary Reading List).

Company manpower planning is the main concern of this text. This is the area of involvement and responsibility and action for senior management. However, junior management with no overall strategic responsibility needs to understand the necessity of relating various personnel activities to an overall policy framework.

The third area of activity relates to the techniques of manpower planning. This text covers these aspects in some detail and sets out the various ones that are available.

It is important to remember that these three are different since the reader may be aware that the term 'manpower planning' applied to such disparate activities can cause confusion. There is little similarity between the work of the Training Commission and the personnel officer engaged in analysing labour turnover but they can both be described as undertaking manpower planning.

The Department of Employment text (reference 1) has defined manpower planning as 'a strategy for the acquisition, utilization, improvement and retention of an enterprise's human resources'.

This definition clearly points to company manpower planning. To avoid confusion, some bodies such as the Institute of Manpower Studies (IMS) have tended to adopt the term 'manpower management' to describe the strategic management of human resources. Of course, the writer of this text is aware that at this level of abstraction, the terms 'manpower' and 'manpower management' which have become widely used denote a range of activities which are remarkably similar to personnel management itself. For many, of course, this so-called 'manpower theme' is intended to apply to the strategic management of human resources which, it has been argued, personnel professionals are ill equipped in training, aptitude and status to handle. It is in response to this suggestion that this text stresses the need for a full contribution from personnel management and this will be returned to later in the 'manpower theme'. There are a number of other essential features of manpower planning and these are set out below.

Integrated policy and practice

Manpower planning seeks to link policy and practice together in day to day decision making; stressing the interrelation of the various areas of personnel management, for example industrial relations, training, development and recruitment. Too frequently these aspects of personnel management have been treated as separate activities. It is important that personnel management is a co-ordinated and integrated activity of management, as is expected of finance, production and marketing.

The effect of today's decisions in the future

Manpower planning is concerned with the future effects of employment decisions made today. This is partly because developing effective managers or craftsmen takes time and therefore decisions about future needs have to be made in advance of the actual requirement. However, manpower planning is also concerned with the more subtle analysis of the long-term effects of decisions. Ceasing apprentice recruitment or making apprentices redundant may save money in the short term but be very costly in the future. That is not to say such decisions should not be made, but at least assessments can be undertaken to determine possible future costs.

Quantification, computers and models
To analyse manpower effectively there must be an effective method of measuring it; and in order to do this it is necessary to classify manpower. It is important to be accurate about numbers of employees, their skills, wastage rates, ages and so on, and it is a prerequisite of any good manpower planning that a reliable information system is established.

'Number crunching' attracted an unfavourable reputation in the early period of manpower planning, partly through lack of numeracy among personnel managers, but also from a recognition that in personnel management many of the important decisions defy quantification. This latter point is crucial, since in personnel management the manager is dealing with the infinite variability of human nature, and in the search for precision, the essential humanity of the subject must not be overlooked.

Tools and techniques
Computers, models and quantification naturally have an important place in manpower planning. The development of such manpower techniques have made a substantial contribution to the understanding of manpower processes and managers need to understand the technical possibilities and limitations. This is now possible through the availability of, for example, the IMS computer model suites. Technical analysis has helped in other areas such as labour turnover where, as a result of understanding the relationship between leav-

ing and length of service, forecasts of leaving can be made and therefore recruitment, training or redundancy can be avoided where appropriate. There are many useful tools and techniques which have been developed through the interest in manpower planning and these are discussed in succeeding chapters.

Information
The feverish search for manpower information and, worse, the ill conceived attempts at computerization, have led to a waste of resources as personnel departments became obsessed with data generation for its own sake. Nevertheless, while recognizing that many important decision areas in manpower planning can only be partly illuminated by data, it is certain that a sound data base is necessary. In providing information and records the computer will undoubtedly be necessary. This is becoming more usual as the use of micros and word processors becomes more widespread.

Supply and demand
In providing a conceptual framework, the ideas of supply (the people available, together with ages, qualifications, leaving rates and so on) and demand (the people required to do the job) were a great aid to a complete understanding of manpower planning. It is largely impossible to make a reliable forecast of levels of demand especially beyond a year or so, though forecasts of supply of people can be more reliable. The problem with the concepts of supply and demand arose with the over-concern for the identification of demand and then the matching of the supply of people to that level of demand.

If not routine matching or mechanical planning, then what? It is in the 'Flexible Firm' that the answer will be found. Furthermore, this will be an answer that is different for every company. Managers must not be diverted from the real task of identifying problems through a close understanding of the company and then formulating flexible strategies for coping with the future as it unfolds.

Manpower planning and corporate planning

Manpower planning is not a self-contained activity. Personnel decisions are made in industrial relations, training, development and recruitment, and are often dealt with as though they are separate activities; it is also argued that the management of people is often tagged on the end of a company decision as though it were some sort of corporate afterthought. As a result the effects of management decisions on employees are often poorly considered. Personnel managers and line managers should attempt to ensure that employment decisions are discussed and assessed at the proper time in the management of day to day company activities. If this is not done, powerful trade unions can force management to reconsider its decision. Unfortunately, this kind of trade union intervention further emphasizes the essentially negative role they often play in industrial affairs.

The contribution of personnel management

The personnel function has undoubtedly progressed a long way since P F Drucker accused it of adopting a firefighting role, but the suspicion still persists that some personnel specialists are in that business for a quiet life and somehow they manage to be disassociated from the messy world of company management. An indication that this view remains true is the lack of discussion amongst many personnel staff of the cost effectiveness of their plans, intentions and indeed of their own existence. Manpower remains the only area of company management where investment decisions of enormous cost can be made with little or no attempt at financial evaluation and post-investment appraisal. The analysis of the personnel department as a force working against company profitability led Peter Townsend in *Up the Organization* to recommend the total disbandment of the personnel department. Figure 3 represents this view of the personnel professional disassociated from company problems of cost, efficiency, productivity and profitability. To be effective, person-

FIGURE 3

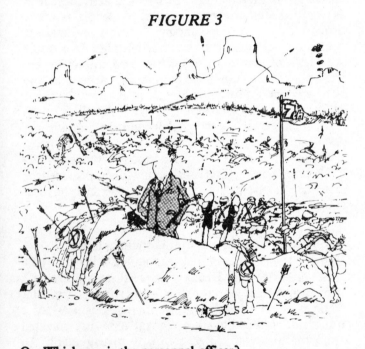

Q   Which one is the personnel officer?
A   He's the one in the middle reflecting on the details of the office Christmas party.

From J T Bramham, *Asian Pacific Conference*, Queensland, 1979 (Reference 60)

nel management must not become divorced from general business management. Increased professional competence must be combined with increased involvement in the company at a high level. Perhaps the increasing number of personnel specialists that are appointed to the directing boards of companies is a sign that many are prepared to become more involved. If this is so, the personnel specialist will soon come to realize that he is not just expected to play an advisory role in management, but is expected to participate fully in the running of a business. There would be no purpose in appointing personnel *directors* if they were not expected to *direct*.

Manpower planning today

In the explanations given above the reader may have observed that definitions referring to 'getting the right people in the right place, at the right time' have been avoided. Manpower planning is not, by and large, the technical scheduling activity such definitions imply although it does have its technical aspects.

The growing strength of personnel departments and of manpower planning within them has already been referred to. No longer is the manpower planner 'looked upon as a curiosity tucked away in the personnel function' (reference 59). The early work in the 1960s of Professor David Bartholomew at the University of Kent at Canterbury, also of Clive Purkiss and others at the Institute of Manpower Studies (IMS) which was publicly launched in 1969 at Sussex University, and the Manpower society founded in 1970 and of course the IPM's own National Committee on Organization and Manpower Planning have all provided impetus in the form of increased awareness of manpower planning and of the techniques available.

Malcolm Bennison (reference 59) in discussing the growth of interest and enthusiasm in manpower plan-

15

ning nevertheless expressed a note of regret when he suggested that opportunities had nevertheless been missed. Instead of dealing with human relations problems, he argued, manpower planning models were built. What began as an aid to foster an increased understanding of parts of the manpower process became treated as the object of the exercise.

Personnel managers did not like the prospect of models and computers, of Markov chains, cohorts, renewal processes, linear programming, optimization, the objective function and stochastic processes, invading the area they had considered safe from technological processes. Up to a point, the commonsense judgement of personnel managers was correct. The early attempts to construct manpower forecasts in great detail were bound to fail. Rare indeed was the attempt at precision and detail necessary since the intention was never to match supply and demand in a methodical way. It is now possible to reflect on these developments. This text will stress the need for two key features. Firstly, a reliable, factual overall view of the organization constantly updated and secondly, flexible manpower policies and strategies to meet and anticipate the changing environment. Therefore, rather than look for 'right' forecasts, the manager should consider a variety of approaches to solve his problems. He might use computers to assist him in reaching decisions by asking questions of the 'what if . . .' variety. This aspect and the use of models is discussed in the relevant chapter in this text.

Appreciation of the importance of planning for employees and of thinking ahead would lead to panic measures such as banning recruitment being rejected since it would be realized that there is no virtue in burning the seed corn to keep it from the rodents. If recruitment had to be stopped, it would be selective. The intention

16

would be to retain the apprentice on a new shorter training period with generalist skills, the technician and the graduate and other skilled employees. If, through necessity, all recruitment was stopped, the cost in the long term would be assessed and the company/board made aware of that cost.

In summary manpower planning encourages the personnel manager to consider manpower issues comprehensively and to consider them strategically. He will seek to develop indicative planning that would be supported by flexible and adaptive control systems through which he would continually update his view of the world. He will also know the areas of greatest return and in seeking support of trade unions will make use of information to formulate a cogent argument.

It was said in the first edition of this text that no country has made much success at employing people in industry without a great deal of waste and loss of human dignity. There are those in academic and political life who tell us that it is already too late and that isolationism, self-containment and central control is the only alternative to chaos. That may be what lies ahead but it seems a poor arrangement to accept if it can be averted. There are, of course, areas of manpower management which remain undeveloped or disappointing in their lack of vision. One example would be the failure to come to terms in a constructive manner with trade unions, and their involvement in the planning and employment process. For the moment progress here has stopped and in any event many people found previous proposals unacceptable. There is also the slow progress towards a coherent manpower policy at national level. However one thing is certain: depression and gloom are not likely to lead to a new dawn. So the manager may as well be optimistic and vigorous in the search for new solutions. This is helped by the greater attention focus-

17

sed on people and employee communication and participation which can help overcome what were considered as intractable manpower problems. We can hope that the heritage of crisis in people relations is not met by another dose of crisis people management.

2 The manpower planning process

This chapter aims to establish a conceptual framework for manpower planning to lead on to the detailed techniques and activities described later in the book. First, a word of caution: it is unlikely that the process represented here can be applied straightforwardly to any given firm. Diagrams of processes tend to suggest a beginning and an end, whereas in practice manpower planning is unlikely to work like that. If it did, it would be tempting to suggest that the activity was not involved in the day to day problems of the firm.

The framework shown in Figure 4 sets out four main phases:

1 investigating — in which an awareness is built up
2 forecasting — when predictions of the future are made
3 planning — when policies to meet the future are agreed
4 utilizing — where the success of the policies is measured.
   Each of these phases has its own subdivision.

The investigation stage looks at the current manpower in the organization, its opportunities and problems, the external environment, productivity and working prac-

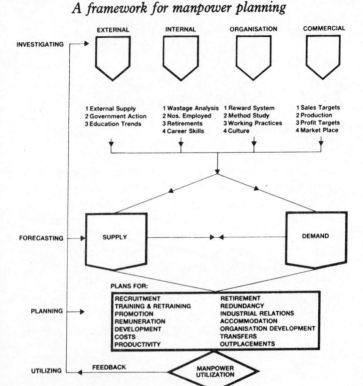

FIGURE 4
A framework for manpower planning

INVESTIGATING	EXTERNAL	INTERNAL	ORGANISATION	COMMERCIAL
	1 External Supply 2 Government Action 3 Education Trends	1 Wastage Analysis 2 Nos. Employed 3 Retirements 4 Career Skills	1 Reward System 2 Method Study 3 Working Practices 4 Culture	1 Sales Targets 2 Production 3 Profit Targets 4 Market Place

FORECASTING — SUPPLY ▶ ◀ DEMAND

PLANNING

PLANS FOR:

RECRUITMENT	RETIREMENT
TRAINING & RETRAINING	REDUNDANCY
PROMOTION	INDUSTRIAL RELATIONS
REMUNERATION	ACCOMMODATION
DEVELOPMENT	ORGANISATION DEVELOPMENT
COSTS	TRANSFERS
PRODUCTIVITY	OUTPLACEMENTS

UTILIZING — FEEDBACK — MANPOWER UTILIZATION

tices and, finally, the organization's financial and marketing intentions.

Forecasting is concerned with demand, which is the requirement for manpower, and supply, which is the provision of that manpower.

Planning and control are concerned with turning forecasts into personnel policies to recruit, train and develop. Good planning strives for flexibility and cohesion, all the policies being interrelated so that they help each other.

20

Utilization is concerned with the final achievement of organizational objectives. These have to be measured in some way, perhaps through costs, productivity or service to the customer.

Throughout the process arrows represent the need to repeat something in the light of what has followed, where problems met at later stages make it necessary to review earlier decisions. They also represent feedback so that the manager knows whether his objectives are being achieved. Thus each stage interrelates and overlaps with others. We can now consider each stage in turn in more detail.

1 Investigating

Before making any forecasts, or plans and policies to meet them, a clear picture of the organization is needed. The effectiveness of planning depends on the detail and accuracy of the information on which it is based. Any failure to grasp the problem at this stage will weaken the whole planning process. It is essential that the various factors affecting the organization, both as opportunities and constraints, are understood and that the problems of present policies and methods ('the way we do things here') are faced. This is not to say that they will be changed, but that they will be recognized as strengths or weaknesses.

Commercial – marketing and finance

If manpower planning is to be effective it must be part of the total business planning of the firm. The business objectives of the firm create the work on which manpower requirements will be based. The organizational analysis will show up strengths and weaknesses in the firm's business plans. Is the firm financially sound? Are competitors reducing our share of the market? What are our objectives in terms of production, sales and

21

profit? How sensitive are we to manpower problems? Is manpower likely to be a problem and might this require a revision of marketing forecasts?

This last point is probably more important now than ever before. Previously managers determined business plans and expected manpower to adjust accordingly either through recruitment or redundancy. As a result of changes mentioned earlier this situation no longer applies. The operation of many firms is now dependent on the supply of manpower. Even if the right numbers of the right kind of employee are available at a price the firm can afford, it may have difficulty in attracting and retaining them.

In firms with a business planning process it is more likely that information will be available to the manager undertaking manpower planning. Often the same manager will be doing both. Where manpower planning is the responsibility of a function not directly represented at board level, problems may emerge. In such a situation the manpower manager is unlikely to be able to influence business plans and will often not be aware of them until a late stage. This situation seems to be changing: many companies now have board members with direct responsibility for manpower management. This results in manpower questions being taken more seriously when 'business' issues like production, sales and profit targets are discussed. There are other manpower problems within corporate planning and these will be referred to later.

To conclude, the sort of factors that should be considered in manpower planning include:

sales forecasts, profit targets, production targets, financial stability, position of competitors, changes in external environment, loss making lines for correction, profit making lines for maximization, social responsibilities of the firm.

Organization – productivity, practices and methods
The analysis of productivity, practices and methods has organizational and individual aspects. The organization may have a particular method of working and if this is changed it will affect manpower. A decision to centralize or decentralize would be an example. Outdated systems of credit control may be updated by computing methods, with a consequent effect on manpower requirements both in terms of the type of manpower required, and the numbers likely to be employed.

It hardly needs saying that these factors are not isolated. Managers, perhaps with an unbecoming reluctance, are realizing that organizational change depends substantially for its success on the good will of the employee. The management of change in its organizational and human aspects is the particular field of study for organization development (OD).

External manpower review
The study of the external environment and its effects on business plans is quite common. Many firms spend large sums of money and other resources to discover the potential market for their products. More recently firms have begun to feel a need to project a favourable public image of the organization itself, often for quite separate purposes than direct selling of a particular product or service. In view of the effort expended in looking at marketing operations it is surprising that, except for occasional local labour market surveys, where manpower is concerned the study of the external environment is poorly developed: this is reflected in the paucity of information available to the manager who tries to undertake such a review.

Increasing interest in manpower management at all levels is leading to efforts to develop knowledge of the external manpower environment: this can take a

23

number of forms. First, there is government manpower policy and its effect on the firm. This is an area which is becoming increasingly significant. While the search for a 'national manpower policy' has proved elusive, the recognition of skills problems has come into the limelight. Unless education and training are structured to meet society's needs in the widest sense industry will suffer. This flexible approach to 'policy' — pragmatic problem solving, rather than the grand design — is the job of the Training Commission as it emerges from the embers of the Manpower Services Commission.

Secondly, the important area for industry is how national and local labour markets develop. The organization needs to know what labour is available now and in the future. It will need to know how it will change following, for example, the increasing numbers of women in employment or fewer young school leavers. In addition to knowledge of numerical aspects, the manager will look to see what skills are available and will be particularly keen to watch for surpluses which he may exploit or shortages which he will anticipate. Such knowledge is particularly valuable when a firm is considering moving. It must be wary of being lured somewhere else by high unemployment only to find that there is a serious shortage of the skills needed.

Thirdly, the manager will want to be aware of the output of the education system. He will be interested in the numbers leaving schools and colleges and will want to know in what way these are changing. Planning will also benefit from an analysis of the disciplines in which potential employees will have been educated at schools, colleges and universities. For instance, a fall in the availability of chemists, chemical engineers or fuel scientists will be significant for many companies.

The provision of places in particular disciplines in the education system is a subject in itself (see Supplementary Reading List). It is perhaps unfortunate that more is not known of industry's requirements before the number of places for various subjects are allocated; certainly education experts are waiting for a clearer expression of industry's needs, though this is not to say that the education system is expected to provide employees solely to the specification of industry — that would be far too narrow a view. But perhaps the student might be equally well educated in a subject more directly useful to his subsequent employer to the benefit of industry, society and the student himself.

Internal manpower review

The knowledge gleaned in this area is particularly important to manpower planning. Other areas are important but often the manager is searching out and taking account of what has been, is being and will be done by others. When studying the internal manpower situation the manager is very close to the development of the plans he is hoping to encourage.

In most organizations the manager can be expected to be hampered by a lack of reliable information about manpower. This will limit the effectiveness of the result but should not prevent the effort taking place. Unless use is made of what is available and its limitations shown it is unlikely that resources will be spent on improvement. The establishment of an information system will be dealt with in more detail in a later chapter.

What is the manager looking for when investigating the current manpower situation? In general terms the purpose is to highlight the opportunities and problems inherent in the manpower employed. The manager will be searching for areas of under-utilization and/or high cost or high turnover. Analyses will be intended to highlight problems arising from the structure of the work force: for instance, where technology has overtaken the skills available amongst employees to exploit it, or where the growth of one departmental activity and the decline of another is not reflected in organizational terms.

Apart from structural problems such as these, there will be a need to look at the employees themselves. At this stage emphasis is less on individual characteristics than on the characteristics of groups. The problems of age distribution are an obvious example. Are the employees predominantly young with consequent problems of promotion, lack of experience and increased wastage? An ageing workforce may indicate retirement problems. Length of service distributions (useful indications of leaving rates), past wastage patterns, skills and qualifications held, promotion policies and past recruitment practices will all highlight manpower opportunities and problems. The manager will be aware that, as he determines the shape of the organization in the future, he will not be able to ignore the internal environment with which he starts. It is less usual but probably of benefit to study the organization in cultural as well as in structural and human terms. By this is meant the style and assumptions on which organizational behaviour is based. The culture will affect the likelihood of certain decisions being made and, once made, that they will be achieved. This field of manpower activity is now seen as part of 'human resources management'.

2 Forecasting

Having established a fund of knowledge on all aspects of the firm's business, it is possible to move to attempts to indicate in which direction manpower is going and in which direction it should go to meet organizational objectives. This distinction is worthy of emphasis. Forecasting is not simply a process of predicting the future. It must spring from a clear intent of where the organization wishes to be.

Even in comparatively developed areas such as marketing, sales, finance and economics, forecasts are endowed with no special prophetic value. Is it all worth the effort? The answer to this question lies in attitudes to forecasting and planning. The point is that the forecasting process throws up problems that may emerge. It will show where the organization is vulnerable or where failure is expensive. The purpose of planning is to provide coherent strategies for various activities. In this way the achievement of forecasts is monitored and problems anticipated or reacted to as the occasion demands. The plan is not fixed but a continually changing frame of reference against which decisions — in this case manpower decisions — are made. Forecasting is concerned with where the organization might be in the future. Even if the forecast is not achieved the manager has an increased awareness for he knows what has been missed, while an efficient control procedure will tell him what he has instead.

Forecasting manpower requirements – demand
The manpower planning process shown at the beginning of this chapter divided forecasting into supply and demand or requirements. First, reference must be made to the use of the words 'requirements' and 'demand'. The problem seems to be that demand may imply a simple identification of workload whereas it is at least as important as workload (and indeed the purpose of requirement forecasting) to gain a knowledge of the type and quality of people the organization should employ. This should not be treated purely as a numerical problem since decisions about the way the organization is to be manned are perhaps more important. In its extreme form the choice may lie between achieving a

given workload either through a labour intensive low skilled workforce, or through a high skilled workforce using the latest capital equipment.

It is worth remembering Smith's warning[22] that the distinction being made between requirements and the supply of those requirements should not be carried too far. It is conceptually a useful distinction to make as it helps understanding but in practice the two are closely related. It is not unusual to start by identifying requirements but the ability to achieve them (supply) must be known or the forecast will be a pious expression of hope with no foundation. In this way supply will affect requirements. Many firms now appreciate this as they have experienced substantial revision of marketing and sales targets due, for instance, to shortages in labour supply.

The forecasting of manpower requirements requires a close knowledge of business plans. The workload aspects, such as sales to be achieved, may be a direct output from business plans into the manpower planning process.

There are various ways of converting work into manpower. Most involve an element of arithmetic even if this is done on the proverbial envelope, but more advanced methods are available. Some of these will be looked at in the chapter on identifying manpower requirements.

Forecasting manpower supply

An obvious and in the short term probably a major way of meeting the requirements for manpower will come from the people currently employed. An important element of the forecasting of supply is therefore concerned with forecasting how many people will leave. Wastage analysis and forecasting (wastage is also often referred to as 'labour turnover') has been well developed as a subject, though more in its statistical than behavioural aspects. To forecast wastage, it is necessary to know about retirements, and forecasts of voluntary wastage. It should be noted that length of service is a useful indicator of leaving. The conventional labour turnover index (often called the BIM (British Institute of Management) labour turnover index or the crude labour turnover index) is often valueless and probably harmful in forecasting. This will be discussed in the chapter on wastage analysis.

Other movements within the organization will result from promotions and transfers and consequently these will require forecasting. First, the potential of employees for promotion will need to be known; secondly, the expectations of employees and the effect of them on promotion rates will have to be assessed.

It will probably be necessary to recruit from outside the organization and this possibility will have to be assessed. A balance must be found between recruiting from outside the organization and internal promotions, weighing the risk of 'in-breeding' against possible disenchantment of existing employees on seeing their own promotion opportunities being lost.

Availability of training resources will affect the supply of labour and so will trade union attitudes and payment policies. No one personnel activity can be excluded from consideration, as failure in one area will undoubtedly affect the others. Employees and their representatives are so important that it may be sensible to involve them in the planning process itself. There must therefore be a clear policy for achieving forecasts through various personnel activities and this is the sphere of planning and implementation.

3 Planning—*control and implementation*
Having assessed the current manpower and business situation and forecast requirements for and supply of

manpower, the manager's attention turns towards the plans needed to ensure that intention is translated into practice.

The purpose of planning is to formulate coherent and interrelated policies designed to achieve the organization's manpower objectives. It is no use embarking on a policy of recruitment if the pay and conditions offered are not competitive or if there are insufficient training resources available.

Planning should imply flexibility and the wider the knowledge and understanding of the organization's manpower strengths and weaknesses the more likely it is that the manager will know how to anticipate or react to the unforeseen.

How can manpower planning help?

In what ways can planning help the manager? Manpower decisions and policies become operational through recruitment, promotion, training and similar personnel activities. Consequently planning will establish the priorities and objectives in these areas. It will also provide knowledge of flexibility if events make it necessary. It is worth listing personnel activities and showing how manpower planning could help them.

Recruitment

A knowledge of future requirements and internal supply of labour is a prerequisite to setting plans for recruitment. It is most important to do this as scarcity, costs and increased skills of manpower prevent an organization from assuming that the right quality and type of manpower will be available.

Training

It is curious that the need to identify requirements for training has not encouraged the development of manpower planning before. Knowledge of manpower intentions will enable plans to be established for training both existing employees (perhaps in new skills) and the new employees being recruited.

Industrial relations
Explicit plans for industrial relations are fairly new to many firms. It was not uncommon for industrial relations to be dealt with in terms of 'crisis management' with insufficient consideration being given to long-term effects. This is now much less the case, for industrial relations — or, perhaps more correctly, 'employee relations' — is the key to personnel activities. Such a view regards the activities as going beyond the negotiating of pay rates and associated working conditions; perhaps, as has already been mentioned, to seeking to achieve greater involvement of the employee in sharing the organization's objectives.

Management and employee development
A knowledge of requirements and supply will indicate likely promotion and development patterns. This should lessen the risk of developing employees for posts that will in the event not exist. Development schemes will also enable alternatives to be highlighted if expected development plans do not materialize. Employee development will also be an input to the planning process as it can indicate the practical limitations for the development of employees.

Pay and conditions
Analysis of the current manpower situation will have indicated where attention to pay and conditions might usefully be concentrated. Relations with business and financial plans will indicate what the firm migh be able to afford.

Manpower costs

Manpower planning provides information on costs as an input but knowledge of requirements and personnel plans to achieve them should enable realistic costings to be made.

Organization development

This is also both an input to and an output from the process. Analysis of the organization structure and culture will highlight likely difficulties, especially where dramatic change is envisaged. Once objectives are determined the OD consultant should know where to concentrate his skills as a change-agent.

Redundancy

It is hoped that a knowledge of requirements and ways of meeting them will prevent the worst of sudden and unexpected reductions in manpower. If manpower is being poorly used it would hardly be surprising for a surplus to be identified. The firm must develop its own policies to meet this situation.

Accommodation and physical requirements

The process should help in developing requirements for office, factory and stores accommodation. As manpower becomes more expensive there will be an increasing need to ensure that employees are not hampered by a lack of materials and equipment.

These are the practical ways in which manpower planning should contribute to better manpower decisions within the firm. Having expressed each activity separately, their interrelation should be emphasized. There is little value in attempting to recruit if pay levels are wrong, if training facilities are not available or if the culture of the organization is not ready for the change implied. Each activity may well depend for success on the achievement of another or others. In this way the purpose of planning is to ensure that policies for each activity link together so that ideally no one offends the direction of another; indeed, each should help the achievements of the others so that the business and ethical objectives of the firm can be met.

4 Utilizing and implementing

If the policies are not implemented and better manpower utilization (however that is measured) is not the result, the exercise will be of little if any value. There is a great deal that can be done (and has been done) in planning at quite low levels in the hierarchy of the firm. Nevertheless, the support of senior management is essential if the way in which day to day decisions are made is to change. Inevitably the effort required to undertake successful manpower planning will be underestimated and it will be difficult to encourage the network of involvement and commitment that is needed.

Measures of utilization will be required. First, the measure will need to be determined. Reduced costs may not be the objective if falling production or poor service to the customer is the result. There is no reason why the measure could not be something relatively altruistic, such as the desire to reduce hours worked or to increase holidays. Measurement of productivity is an area that is well covered elsewhere in management literature (see for example reference 39). The organization must decide what its criteria for success are and develop a system for ensuring that they are achieved.

Throughout this description of the manpower planning process the emphasis has been on flexibility and the flow of information from one phase to another.

This interrelationship is important. It is perfectly feasible to undertake a manpower exercise, such as wastage, in isolation but if the problems that emerge are to be solved it is inevitable that other factors become involved. For example, an analysis of a high labour turnover problem may highlight overmanning (perhaps the employees are bored with having insufficient interesting work to occupy them), or undermanning. Perhaps wage rates are failing to keep pace with competitors and need to be revised. Recruitment methods may be at fault; as a result the wrong people are employed in the first place. The problem may be far reaching and suggest wider problems of organization and management.

This interrelationship is at the heart of manpower planning. The organization is viewed as a system where action in one area has an effect elsewhere. This is why recruitment and training decisions cannot be dealt with separately. The implementation of one leads to a need for the other.

These relationships are of course not static and neither is the environment in which they exist. Continuous and rapid change results in no 'plan' in any simple mechanistic sense being relevant for very long. Manpower planning is in practice a flow of information through which the manager may develop increasing awareness of manpower problems and opportunities in the organization. Through this awareness he is better placed to develop with his colleagues co-ordinated personnel policies for the organization which enable it to meet its economic objectives while fulfilling its social responsibilities.

3 Identifying manpower requirements

There is a relative lack of attention given to analysing manpower requirements (though management services specialists might disagree) and it is important that a coherent framework be developed. Crucial manpower decisions are made at this stage (or perhaps not made!). For example, the decision to expand into new markets or build new plants may depend for success on correctly identified manpower requirements.

Manpower requirements are not only concerned with numbers but more importantly with type and quality. For instance, the decision to have craftsmen trained through adult modules or an apprenticeship, or the need for qualified and high calibre managers or the use of technicians are all highly important manpower policy decisions. Many will have important cost elements (graduate trainee schemes are expensive) while others will have a highly charged political element (the decision to reduce or dispense with apprenticeships or to switch from a labour intensive process to a capital intensive high technology process). This is the area where the important manpower policy decisions are made and where most stumbling blocks to improved performance probably lie. It is also where the rewards for success are probably greatest. Nevertheless these are essentially demand decisions and the manager, and especially the personnel manager, should be involved in making them.

Problems of a mechanistic approach
One difficulty might be the use of the word 'demand' and the misuse in manpower planning of statistical techniques where this has suggested that manpower requirements can be forecast by determining some relationship and then projecting it into the future. There are numerous examples of estimating requirements by relating employees to units of output. This chapter is purposely entitled 'identifying manpower requirements', for in demand analysis and forecasting the purpose is not to estimate workload but to estimate how many employees are required to meet that workload.

Although there is rarely a neat distinction it is useful to think of the process being divided into the first two phases given in Figure 4, that is investigating and forecasting. While an element of prediction will be essential the manager is probably right to suspect that although he may have problems in the future he has as many in the present. As well as not knowing what manpower is required in the future he may not know what numbers and types of manpower he should be employing now (ie opposed to those actually employed).

Before going further another distinction should be made. The manager has to distinguish between a 'need' which is essential and a 'need' which is 'nice to have'. Human nature being what it is there will be a fair amount of needs based on nice to have and these will have to be adjudicated.

Investigating manpower demand
Before it is possible to forecast manpower requirements, it is essential that the manager should understand the employment process in the firm.[19]

36

Involvement in, or at least knowledge of, business planning is vital. The manager should know what problems the firm has and what major impending changes there are so that he can express them in manpower terms. Unfortunately, business decisions are often taken with insufficient knowledge of the impact on the people employed, with possibly wasteful consequences.

Manpower demand decisions are not only concerned with the long-term future. On investigation many managers may find themselves asking why a particular piece of work is undertaken by employees in such numbers and with particular skills. Consequently, there are a number of questions that should be asked at this stage. These are:

1 does the work need to be done?
2 are the correct numbers of employees doing it?
3 have the employees the requisite skills?
4 could investment (say in machinery) reduce total costs or are there other ways and means of carrying out the work?

1 Does the work need to be done?
The first question concerns the need to do the work. This may query the validity of the marketing and production objectives of the firm and there is no reason why these should not be examined. Such objectives are not inviolate, unchallengeable edicts. In any event whether work is needed may be questioning custom and practice rather than fundamental objectives. This will take the form of anything from outdated maintenance schedules to the completion of documents that nobody uses, or simply procedures that create work by their inefficient operation.

Systems and procedures tend to last longer than the purpose for which they were intended, which is why the manpower demand analysis needs to question whether the work is needed at all. It is worth noting that poor productivity may result not from poor individual effort but from wasteful tasks. In time, of course, the employee becomes aware of the wasteful nature of his task and the debilitating effect this has on his confidence may well result in a reduction in his individual performance. It is perhaps unfortunate that managers have not generally been able to harness the individual employee's good sense and creativity as a test of the usefulness of the work he is doing.

The questioning of whether a particular task needs to be done or whether it is done in the most productive way is simply stated but the difficulty of doing it should not be underestimated in practice. The manager who attempts this will find himself challenging value judgements (including his own) about particular operations and facing the considerable inertia that surrounds established practices.

2 Are the correct numbers of employee's doing it?

Various methods are available to managers to determine if a particular operation is under-or overmanned. Method and work study are established ways though perhaps not regarded as favourably as they once were. Comparisons with other plants, factories or departments are alternative methods which, while not necessarily highlighting the 'best', will probably bring out the 'worst'. The manager will not be constrained by current practice, because improvements in the skill of current employees may be one way of improving employee performance and the use of machinery may be another. Trends in productivity and utilization which are gained in this way will be useful at the forecasting stage.

3 Have the employee's the requisite skills?

The failure to provide employees with sufficient training in industry has long been recognized. The improvement of training was the central purpose of the Industrial Training Act of 1964. The establishment of training boards and levy grant was designed to encourage or coerce employers to implement more training. The success of the training boards has no doubt been limited by some employers' lack of commitment to the ideal and by the lack of a clear idea of requirements before training took place. The employer was not committed because he did not see the lack of skills as central to his manpower and business problems. In undertaking manpower planning the analysis and forecasting of requirements will help the manager see more clearly the need to add to his employees' stock of skills and hopefully justify the expense of it in terms of the return of his investment. Rapid changes in methods and technology increase the possibility of employees' skills being outdated. Only repeated and rigorous investigation will enable problem areas to be identified and resolved before they become serious (and even before they occur).

4 Could investment reduce total costs?

The manager will be concerned with identifying areas where capital equipment will help the employee do his job better or more efficiently. He may also be able to reduce the number of employees by using more capital or alternatively maintain employment but increase output. The manager will also wish to bear in mind which jobs could be undertaken by machinery if, for instance, the necessary supply of manpower was not available and alternative methods had to be used even at enhanced costs. The importance of financial investment to manpower questions suggests that a closer

39

relationship might usefully be developed between personnel and finance departments.

Forecasting manpower requirements

A knowledge of the present situation on manpower requirements is essential if a satisfactory forecast is to be made.

Often decisions are taken in other fields such as capital investment in new processes or mergers or changes in technology, with limited consideration being given to manpower implications. This is not to suggest that human considerations should necessarily deter progress but that, unless manpower aspects are given their full weight, the project as a whole may disappoint the hopes held for it. Many firms have discovered through wasted investment in computers how important it is that employees are committed to the change to which the installation will lead.

The personnel manager's position in the firms hierarchy is important. If he is not on the board he will find it difficult to affect policy decisions which have considerable effect on the need for manpower. And presence on the board is useless if the personnel manager does not have the professional attitude and expertise necessary, backed up by competent staff, to make an effective contribution.

Linked to this is the fact that the work to be done and the manpower required to do it will come from the firm's marketing, production and financial objectives. In some firms these objectives will be explicitly stated and will reduce some of the confusion in trying to determine manpower requirements and subsequent policy. It will not be unusual if the manager has to identify requirements without a clear knowledge of the objectives, either because there are none explicitly stated or because he has not been informed of them.

For the manager who is determined to make progress there are a number of pointers which should help him approach the problem, and these are described in the following paragraphs.

Time-scale of forecasts.
The time-scale over which he intends to analyse and forecast is one area he must consider.[19]. It will depend largely on the nature of the decision to be affected. Figure 5 shows that different time-scales of forecasts have different purposes. In the shorter term the manager will be concerned with budgeting and the need to prepare expenditure targets up to two years ahead. In this time his ability to change the make-up and structure of the labour force will be limited to tactical recruitment or training plans.

His medium and longer term forecast of between two and seven years opens up the possibility of greater changes resulting from new manpower policies such as decisions to make greater use of apprenticeships or graduate entrants. Although related to the future the recruitment decision may well have to be made today.

Though few organizations attempt forecasting beyond seven years, this period would make it possible to think in terms of changing the entire structure and quality of the labour force. Although such a long time-scale is frightening, it is the one against which decisions to make major changes in, say, managerial manpower have to be made.

Manpower planning is concerned more naturally with medium and long-term planning and forecasting because major planned changes can be affected over longer time scales. Generally we are not concerned here with short-term forecasting or budgeting except as a means of ensuring that longer term targets are achieved. Manpower planning is concerned with

41

FIGURE 5

Time scale of manpower forecasts

	BASIS OF REQUIREMENT	BASIS OF AVAILABILITY	POSSIBLE ACTIONS
0 – 6 months	Current budget	Current manpower plus temporaries	Contractors overtime recruitment redundancy
6 – 18 months	Forward budget	Current manpower less projected leavers	Promotion transfer recruitment flexible working
18 months – 5 years	Forward budgets and plans	Projected current manpower plus those completing training	Flexible jobs recruitment planned rundown training programmes
more than 5 years	Predicted market and technological changes	Expected labour market and education system supplies	Organization development and job restructuring management development programmes

today's decisions since unless decisions are made now an opportunity to affect the future may be lost.

The time-scale to which the manager is planning his manpower will be determined by the nature of the decision he wishes to affect and the environment in which the organization finds itself. It is useless to come forward with five to seven year development plans if the firm's problems threaten to engulf it within months. Problems could be the result of the firm's previous actions or may follow from external influences largely out of its own control.

An important factor which determines time-scale in relation to forecasts is the time needed to train and develop a particular type of employee. Consequently, engineers who may take three to five years to develop and train will require a forecast covering a similar period. A job for which an employee can become effective more quickly after recruitment, or for whom special training is not required, will require a shorter term forecast. When the range of skills in industry was smaller, technology less complex and manpower plentiful, managers could expect to respond to demand quickly by recruiting in the open market. Up to a point this is still possible but the manager would be unwise to rely upon it as his sole strategy. Consequently, he will use his forecasts to look at requirements in areas where a long lead time in training or recruitment results in a need to know in advance what the organization's manpower requirements are.

One further point can be added. Forecasting usually consists of associating certain events with a certain point in time in the future.

This is not always necessary. It will be valuable to know that a certain event may occur and what its effect on manpower employment will be. This may be necessary where the likelihood of an event happening is high but it is not known when this will be. Alternatively, the manager may consider situations that he does not expect will arise, but prefers to work out contingency solutions so that, if they do, he can react or anticipate sensibly.

Finally it should be noted that time scales are not absolute. Needs will differ from organization to organization. Apart from those mentioned above, factors which will influence the forecast are the size of the company, the industry or market in which it is engaged and whether it is regarded as a career organization or whether employees move on after a short period.

Rate of change and product time-cycle

In preparing forecasts the manager will know the needs of the product for which he is determining manpower requirements. A firm concerned with a seasonal product or with a short time-cycle will need different forecasts from one which is dealing with the development and exploitation of expensive capital projects.

The rate of change being experienced will affect forecasting, a changing environment being more difficult to manage than a stable one. Consequently, in a changing environment a manager will be trying to increase his range of control by more accurate statements of future intentions and their effect upon manpower. In practice, this will probably result in forecasts with a shorter time-span, since the greater the rate of change the less reliable and probably less useful longer-term forecasts become.

Detail of forecast required

The need for increased control will probably necessitate greater detail in the forecast itself. One of the purposes of a forecast is to know where the unforeseen is occurring. Clearly many events will occur which were not

44

foreseen but neither are they of any consequence. The manager will forecast only the detail which may significantly affect his ability to do a task needed to meet organizational objectives.

The types of occupations being forecast will affect the need for detail. It is probably necessary to forecast each discrete level of manpower for which different training, recruitment and other programmes are required. This means that it may not be necessary to distinguish in the forecast between a clerk in one section and a clerk in another if the skills are similar and relatively transferable. On the other hand, it will be necessary to distinguish forecasts of managers who are accountants from managers who need to be engineers: in this case different training and development programmes will result in an employee who is not easily transferable to the other job.

Forecasting is unlikely to be that simple. Many firms may have accountants doing engineering jobs or vice versa. Consequently, when building up the forecast from jobs it will not always be straightforward to identify the type of person required. For instance, when considering a group of jobs such as the board it may not be considered necessary for any particular one of the director jobs to be filled by an accountant or an engineer. The firm may reasonably decide that any one of the jobs could be undertaken adequately by an employee who happens to have an engineering background. However, it may be unacceptable that all the directors be engineers. In many cases, therefore, in the forecast of requirements it is not essential that all jobs are filled by employees with specific skills. There may well be a range of skills. The organization will be seeking a degree of balance and availability across a range of skills and attributes.

Importance of assumptions

Before considering some of the statistical approaches to forecasting the importance of assumptions that underlie the forecast should be stressed. These assumptions should, of course, be made explicit so that the forecast can be judged against them. Assumptions can cover a variety of items though in manpower terms; some important ones are:

> sales and/or services to be achieved, production targets, trade union attitudes to proposals, external economic and social factors, productivity trends and factors affecting utilization, relationships between work and men, relationships upon which forecasts are given statistical treatment.

The manager must be aware of the assumptions that are built into statistical techniques and these should be made explicit. There is often a problem here and if the statistics are complex the statistician should ensure that the manager agrees with the assumptions that are implicit in the forecast.

This situation will tend to arise where complex computer models are developed faster than the manager's ability to understand the assumptions going into them. The result is likely to be unfortunate, either because the method is not used and a valuable aid is wasted or the manager blindly accepts what is 'forecast' from the machine without exercising his judgement. The manager has every advantage to gain in using statistics and he and the professional statistician will be wary of using them improperly.

Quantitative approaches to forecasting

Having determined the background against which forecasts are to be made the manager can consider which of a number of processes are useful to him. In many ways forecasting is a process of determining what can be estimated, what can be calculated, what is taken as given and what has to be guessed. The manager will not expect to remove the necessity for guesswork, though it is to be hoped that his 'guesses' will gradually become intelligent judgements based on common-sense experience and the best information available. These are four basic approaches to forecasting manpower requirements:

1 use of workload factors
2 use of time trends or time-series
3 use of relationships and ratios of productivity
4 managerial judgement

Before looking at each in turn it should be mentioned that, though listed separately, they are not necessarily mutually exclusive. The use of workload factors may well be supported by relationships and ratios of productivity and time trends. All three will require a fair helping of managerial judgement.

1 Use of workload factors
It is often helpful to think of workload when considering manpower requirements. It is an expression that managers generally find easy to understand as they use it when considering manpower problems. It also allows work to be expressed in terms of units other than men required (such as man hours). It is easier to calculate the effect on a particular category of work of, say, capital investment in new machinery. The conversion into employees is then undertaken as a demand activity.

Basically, the workload factor method means separating the work to be done into its discrete parts, (ie the forecasts do not confuse the installation of central heating, which will take a few days, with the installation of a cooker, which will take a few minutes). Each part is

47

then forecast and converted into manning requirements by a conversion factor. This might be the number of man hours required to do each job which can be multiplied by the number of jobs and thus the total requirement for man hours obtained. It is not difficult to convert this into employees required.

FIGURE 6
Using the workload method

(i) Classify work

Meters	hours per job – 0.5
Installation	– 2.2
Maintenance	– 1.6
Emergency	– 1.1

(ii) Forecast work in jobs 000s

	89	90	91
Meters	12	13	10
Installation	95	104	123
Maintenance	29	34	38
Emergency	8	6	5

(iii) Convert into man hours 000s

	89	90	91
Meters	6	7	5
Installation	209	229	271
Maintenance	46	54	61
Emergency	9	7	6
TOTAL	270	297	343

(iv) Convert into men required assuming 1,800 hours/man

	89	90	91
Employees	150	165	191

An example of the workload method is shown in Figure 6. Certain problems arise with the use of this method:

(a) not all work will be capable of expression in this way

(b) standard times for jobs may not be widely available and may depend on the penetration of work study schemes

(c) the standards for the job may be based more on tradition and expectation rather than on a logical assessment of what is possible. This may be especially true where standards are negotiated and therefore become politically charged

(d) it may be difficult to give proper allowance to a saving resulting from capital investment

(e) over a period standards may become slack and may not represent a good base for forecasting.

The method should therefore be used with caution for forecasting beyond one to three years, though if it draws attention to problem areas and need for change it can still be of value.

2 *Use of time trends or time-series*

An alternative method is to analyse employment levels over a time (a time-series) and use this as a basis for forecasting manpower levels. This will mean projecting the past into the future and then allowing for any foreseen changes resulting in a change in use of capital and machinery, change in external economic climate, internal problems within the firm and emergence of competitors.

The employment levels, when recorded over a period, will potentially reveal five distinct elements shown in Figure 7:

(a) *a trend,* as shown in Figure 7a, is a gradual and regular increasing or decreasing level of employ-

49

FIGURE 7
Time series

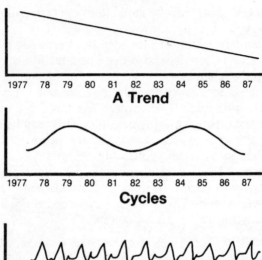

A Trend

Cycles

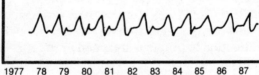

Seasonal Fluctuations

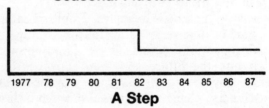

A Step

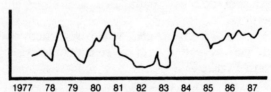

Random Fluctuations

ment, probably over some years

(b) *cyclical effects*, as shown in Figure 7b is a gradual and repeated upward and downward movement over a period. This may well be associated with some particular event, such as economic activity in the country generally

(c) *seasonality*, as shown in Figure 7c, will occur only when more than one time point per annum is recorded. It will record the different level of activity between, say, winter and summer

(d) *a step*, as shown in Figure 7d, is a sudden change in the level of employment which will probably accompany some identifiable change in the environment, such as a cutback/increase in sales or introduction of new machinery

(e) *random fluctuations*, as shown in Figure 7e, is a series of changes in levels of employment that do not follow any obvious pattern. In this case techniques, such as the 'moving average' will help to highlight any trend and suggest the amount of possible error in the forecast.

The trends shown in Figure 7 are simpler to determine than will usually be the case. In practice they will probably all be happening at the same time. Care must consequently be taken when interpreting the information. For example, a distinction needs to be made between a sharp change in employment being a once and for all step or a random fluctuation. Identification of the cause will help to determine which it is. Also, one has to distinguish between events that resulted in a change and will recur and those that will not. Finally, events which are to take place in the future will need identifying and their potential effect on the projected employment level assessed. The forecast must not become a sterile extrapolation of what occured previously.

Other considerations, such as the possibly confusing

51

effect on employment levels of the use of overtime or contractors, or 'built in surplus', will need to be watched. An observed stable level of employment may be due to the use of overtime and contractors to shave peaks rather than due to any inherent stability in the requirement for manpower. There are a number of ways of forecasting from such an analysis. The forecast can be projected by 'eye', that is, by estimating the direction of the line into the future.

Other methods and detailed explanations are available from the references at the end of this book (see, for example, 14 and 19).

Other problems with which the manager will be confronted will concern the amount of historical data that should be used, whether it is relevant (and whether it exists). He will have difficulty in assessing the effect of previous changes and perhaps greater difficulty with future changes. A further problem will be the expected accuracy of the forecast. Clearly the further into the future the forecast goes, the more likely it is that statistical error will increase. This will be especially true where the projection relies heavily on past trends. Finally, it is usually regarded as inappropriate to use analyses of time series for forecasting beyond three years; consequently the method is more applicable to short and medium than to long-term forecasting. Uncertainty about the future probably makes this remark true of all methods. Beyond three years general trends only are possible.

Using time-series – employment levels
Here the manager graphs past employment levels and uses the time series to forecast where employment will go in the future. Important judgements will have to be made: is the level of business activity the same as before, and have there been changes in the environ-
52

FIGURE 8
Manpower employed trends

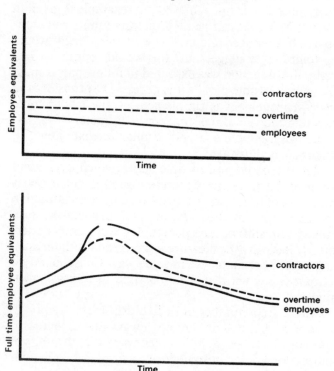

ment? what has been the use of overtime and contractors and how would that effect employment levels? Is the level of overtime appropriate and how would a changed level affect manpower requirements?

In each case the manager will have to make a judgement about the effect on future employment levels. Often he will be able to refer to past occurrences of the same event and estimate its effect. Sometimes he will have to use stated objectives (that a reduction of a certain percentage of manpower justifies a piece of capital investment). In all cases he will require judgement either to prepare the forecast or to consider contingencies if it is not achieved. An example is given in Figure 8; here it can be seen that the number of employees has reduced and on this evidence alone it would be tempting to suggest that this would continue, especially if production was expected to follow past trends. To avoid possible pitfalls it is necessary to consider the ways management is supplementing the labour force through the use of overtime and contractors.

In this example a 'trend' similar to that shown in Figure 7 is illustrated.

An alternative use of time series which overcomes some of the problems of forecasting employment levels is the use of trends in productivity. The main attraction is that the method is simple that units produced/man/shift or sales per employee are easily understood. Basically the measure is concerned with measuring output per employee in some way. Consequently if output is known it will be possible to forecast manpower.

There are a number of difficulties. First, 'improvements' in productivity are not always due to increased human effort. Secondly, it is necessary that the units of output are known in some form. Thirdly, the relationship between output and employees may not be straightforward. For instance, increases in output may lead to economies (or wasteful excesses) of larger scale operations. Fourthly, factors intended to increase productivity (such as new machinery or a bonus scheme) may not have the expected effect, or will work only over a limited period before the situation reverts to previous patterns, but at a higher level of expense.

It may not be possible to relate output to one all-important factor. It often happens that a number of factors play an interrelated and complicated part making forecasting difficult. Statistical techniques such as multiple regression analysis are available to undertake this sort of work.

Finally, a difficulty will arise as many employees cannot be related to output in a direct way. It may be difficult to measure their work; other standards will have to be established. These need not be arbitrary and some organizations have been able to establish satisfactory relationships between various factors such as personnel staff per 100 employees or secretaries per 10 managers employed.

3 Use of relationships and ratios of productivity

The productivity method of forecasting manpower involves relating one factor with another, either to forecast workload and then use this to forecast manpower or to forecast manpower directly. If trends are not to be used the manager must know what is to happen to some of the variables which affect employment.

The easiest method is to establish a direct relationship between manpower and the work to be done. If an assessment of future work to be done (perhaps available from marketing objectives) is available it is then possible to use this to forecast the manpower required. The forecast relies on past relationships continuing into the future and this will often not be so. The manager will therefore have to use his judgement to determine how it may change. An example of using this method is given in Figure 9. It is known that each salesman can achieve £10,000 worth of sales; as sales are known manpower levels required can be forecast. The relationship between unit sales and manpower can be 'drawn by eye' or assessed more accurately using a statistical technique such as regression analysis.

FIGURE 9
Salesmen forecast from known sales value

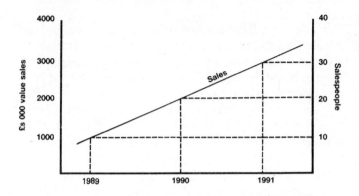

More often it may be necessary to identify requirements in stages by raising a forecast of jobs and then
relating that through some measure of productivity to
the manpower required; an example is given in Figure
10(a) and (b). In this example a relationship is established between the appliances in use and the service
jobs this leads to as customers request maintenance for
their appliances. The forecast of appliances in use can
be derived from sales forecasts and market surveys and
this can be used to indicate the jobs which must be
completed in the future. In Figure 10(a) the forecast of
jobs is shown by the dotted lines read off against the
'service jobs' axis.

The next stage is to establish the relationship between men and jobs; this is shown in Figure 10(b).
Information available for 1986-8 indicates that a rise in
jobs leads, as would be expected, to an increase in employees required. By projecting this line into the future it
is possible to read off the men required to complete a
certain number of jobs. In this case the jobs forecast for
1989 and 1990 obtained in Figure 10(a) is used to read

56

FIGURE 10(a)*

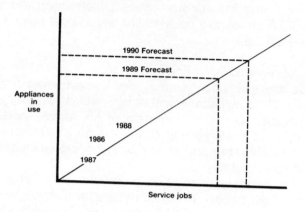

off employees required on the horizontal axis. The problem is that forecasts are being used to develop other forecasts. Consequently it is essential to observe caution, especially if the results seem odd to the manager.

FIGURE 10(b)

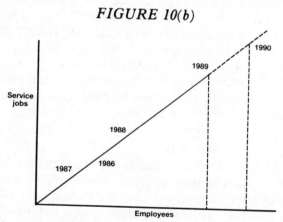

* The examples given here and elsewhere are intended for illustrative purposes only

Comparing the performance of one plant, department or section is another use of productivity measures. Any differences can be discussed and a target manning level agreed.

4 Managerial judgement

The manager can, of course, base his manpower decisions on his own judgement of what will occur, though he should add to the strength of his judgement by looking at and analysing all the available information and making appropriate use of statistical techniques and statistical advice.

It is surprising how much information is available in other departments that could be used for planning purposes if its existence and usefulness was generally recognized. For instance, capital investment programmes in the finance department, or marketing and sales objectives and targets in the marketing department, may well be valuable indicators of future need for manpower.

It is possible to use a method of structured judgement by which a number of managers are asked to make forecasts of requirements. Each manager is then given the forecasts of other managers and asked to change his own. In this so-called Delphi method, managers change their assessment when they see assessments of others. In this way all experience is pooled, a consensus emerges and the worst excesses are avoided.

Working back from costs

Working backwards to manpower requirements from costs is another method worth examining. With the help of the finance department the manager should be able to work out what the organization can afford to spend if profit and market targets are to be met. This gives a good indication of manpower requirements because the manager then has to plan for a workforce capable of achieving the work to be done within a cost constraint. This is an attractive method which deserves further development. It has the supreme advantage that, in working from the future to the present, the manager is not unnecessarily constrained by past practices which have probably been inefficient, though human reaction to his proposals should not be ignored.

The manager must also make judgements on future managerial requirements. Most methods dealing with productivity methods or output are unlikely to be of direct benefit. It is possible that managerial requirements can be built on to the forecasts of other categories, though it is more likely that the manager will have to make judgements about the numbers of managers in various grades and on qualities and abilities they should have. In this area of design of managerial structures models can be particularly useful. The manager is able to look at and consider the opportunities and problems of certain sorts of organization and analyse the problems of achieving them. The degree of judgement in assessing requirements is particularly marked in managerial occupations because the factors leading to the need for them are complex and largely unquantifiable. Although this is so, the effort to find relationships between growth in managerial and staff manpower and other events may well be fruitful. It may be possible to relate personnel officers to total manpower, making suitable allowances for changes in the level of activity resulting from, say, increased or reduced recruitment or training. It may be possible to compare one plant or department with another: if one plant seems to have a larger number of senior managers, personnel officers or operational researchers, it can be investigated to ascertain whether any worthwhile benefits emerge from the additional cost.

Another way at looking at managerial or professional manpower requirements is to study the work that is being undertaken to determine whether professional skills are necessary — other than as a way of increasing the salary level for the job. It is often useful to question managers who employ such professionals on why they are needed. Why was a particular recruitment decision made and on what assumptions about future need was it based?

The techniques should be used by the manager though he must be aware of their limitations. Discredit comes to statistics and manpower planning from the misuse and not the proper use of statistics and other quantitative applications. The 'statistical approach' is often criticized on the wrong assumption that this implies the exclusion of other contributions. Indeed, in the area of demand forecasting, the range of complexities is so great that it is difficult to see how in the long run the use of statistics as a way of handling the variety of probabilities can be avoided.

It is perhaps worthwhile clarifying the basic weakness of many approaches presented here. They may well help in estimating craft requirements or the need for salesmen but the real demand decision in manpower planning may be whether craftsmen are the appropriate form of manpower, or whether a staff graded technician is not needed instead. This task of identifying qualitative requirements for manpower is the most important demand decision, and statistical techniques should be used as appropriate. The manager must question the current manning arrangements and look for more effective methods. This is the purpose and benefit from demand manpower planning.

To end this chapter it is worth setting out the problems that have been discussed.

Problems in demand forecasting

uncertainty about the future
relying on the past by uncritical extrapolation
lack of data on workload past and present
difficulty in making assumptions
lack of integration with corporate planning
mechanistic approach — reliance on statistics
need for forecasting not appreciated by management
trying to do too much (use what is available)

These difficulties can be overwhelming and for this reason flexibility in 'supply' (the people we have or can get) will be crucial.

4 Analysing manpower supply—I

Having considered the need for manpower it is necessary to test that it is available. Before going further the note of caution made earlier should be re-stated: in practice supply and demand will not separate neatly as chapter divisions might suggest. Although feedback is important in a planning process, and will allow plans and forecasts at all stages to be reviewed and revised, in practice the manager needs to be aware of limitations on the supply of manpower when determining his requirements (or indeed when setting marketing and financial objectives) and of the consequences of ignoring behavioural aspects such as motivation, employee aspirations and job enrichment.

In recent years a great deal of effort has been put into analysing and forecasting the supply of manpower. In view of the increasing constraints on management in recruiting, retaining and dispensing with employees this is hardly surprising. It is not all that long ago that management could reasonably expect to find in the labour market an amenable work force in sufficient numbers and with the requisite skills. Once recruited the employee was pleased to have a job and would carry it out with at least respectable diligence. If on the other hand the manager had surplus manpower or simply did not care for an individual, he could terminate his employment. The initiative lay with the manager. It is hardly surprising that limited impetus was given to planning manpower and as a result such a sad inheritance in industrial relations built up.

Today, the initiative rests increasingly with the employee, or rather with organized groups of employees. Technology has increased the skill and therefore scarcity of many jobs and at the same time reduced others to levels of excruciating boredom: the first effect makes recruitment difficult while the second creates problems of retention once the employee is recruited. Time and the scale of unemployment and social security benefits had blunted some of the fear of unemployment, while changing social conditions in an increasingly complex society create still greater problems of manpower supply. Time and continued industrial difficulties will no doubt create new problems.

In the meantime the manager must concentrate on a rigorous examination of the supply of manpower before he needs it if he is to make sure it is likely to be available. What approaches might usefully be adopted?

The manager is attempting to find out who he employs now and how these employees may develop in the future. Attempts to do this often concentrate on counting manpower strengths but it is also important to analyse, forecast and subsequently manage the movements of manpower, since it is through recruitment, promotion and training that manpower requirements are achieved.

Analysis of current manpower employed
Counting and classifying the employees in the organization is an important first step. Unfortunately records are often so poor that this is more difficult than it ought to be. Since the purpose of manpower planning is to

co-ordinate strategies for achieving manpower objectives, it follows that manpower must be counted in categories that can be converted into meaningful recruitment, training, industrial relations and other manpower policies. Consequently employees must first be classified into discrete categories so that clerks are not mixed up with engineers or accountants with salesmen. The problems of occupational classification will be discussed in the chapter on information required for manpower planning, which can be surprisingly limited.

An obvious source of the supply of future needs for some time ahead at least will be the manpower employed now. Consequently the manager will attempt to ascertain the strengths and weaknesses of current employees. This will take a number of forms, such as analyses of distribution of age, sex, length of service, promotion patterns, skills and qualifications and wastage. It will be necessary to separate the organization into its various discrete parts such as by department and by occupation. If this is not done in sufficient detail, a serious problem in one department or occupation may be masked by a generally satisfactory situation in other departments. This implies a heavy commitment of effort. Consequently it is prudent to select certain areas and concentrate on them, rather than attempting to cover everything at once. In selecting the area for attention two factors should be considered. First, it is a good idea to identify those manpower areas which are most crucial to the effectiveness of the organization: Secondly, effort should be concentrated on the manager's problems. This is particularly sound advice to aspiring manpower planners. Many manpower studies have lain unused because they dealt with areas of personal interest to the 'planner' or which he perceived as problems rather than with the pressing problems with which the manager was trying to cope.

FIGURE 11
Analysis of age distribution

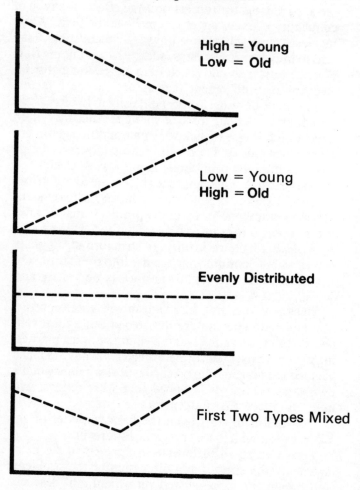

High = Young
Low = Old

Low = Young
High = Old

Evenly Distributed

First Two Types Mixed

Age distribution

There are a number of reasons why it is important to analyse age distributions. Age determines retirement levels and will indicate whether sufficient younger people are available for succession. Age effects the type of contribution an employee can make to the firm. While increasing age will reduce physical effectiveness, may lead to higher sickness rates, and perhaps limit the flow of new ideas, it should also lead to increasing maturity, stability and judgement (age is not the only factor: morale may be more important than it is often supposed; also, a labour force of young females may often have a higher rate of sickness than middle-aged men. How much this is due to differences in sex or differences in the jobs being done is not always clear).

The manager will want to highlight the age distribution problems of his employees so he may take remedial action or simply be aware of the problems that he faces if his opportunities for action are limited. He will seek to achieve a balance in the age structure of his employees and to continue that balance into the future. The matter of what constitutes balance is not easily answered.

An ageing force may be an advantage where contraction and redundancies are threatened but a disadvantage if the organization wants a young, vibrant marketing image. Consequently the manager will have to make his own judgement as to what constitutes balance in his own organization. It is hoped that what follows will help him make that judgement.

It is useful to start from the basic varieties of age distribution which are shown in Figure 11.

Too often age distributions are presented for management with little if any discussion of the problems and opportunities associated with them, still less any attempt to indicate what might be done in practice. The

FIGURE 12 (a)
All employees

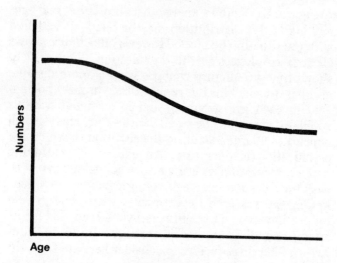

FIGURE 12(b)
Managers

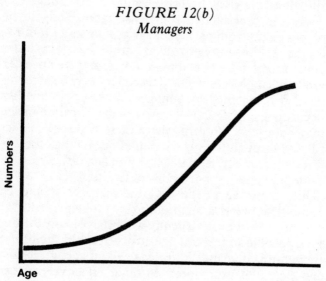

following example suggests ways in which the practising personnel officer can do this.

Figure 12(a) shows an age distribution. A manager looking at this distribution may be relatively satisfied with the situation he faces. However, this figure shows all staff employees in the organization. Figure 12(b) shows how the picture changes when a more discrete graph is drawn. This figure shows the number of managers in each age grouping and immediately various problems emerge. The significance of any analysis will depend to a large extent on the situation in which the organization is operating. An expanding marketing based organization entering a new technology may well wish for a predominance of younger people in its marketing and research departments, where energy and innovation are at a premium and yet be satisfied for its established divisions to be managed by older employees. The three factors to consider here are first, the situation in which the organization is operating, secondly the characteristics that are more likely to be predominant from particular age groupings and, thirdly, the relationship between age groupings. This latter point might take two forms. For example, an older group of employees in one department may be acceptable if it is matched by younger employees in another department. Alternatively two groups disparate in age may only be a problem where there is direct contact such as through the supervision of one by the other. If difference in age is matched by major differences in value systems, supervision difficulties may result. While analysing in this way the manager should be looking for practical solutions to the problem identified and also how the age structure will behave in the future. It is possible to forecast age structures into the future though this demands knowledge about age of recruits and potential promotions to do it effectively. Most

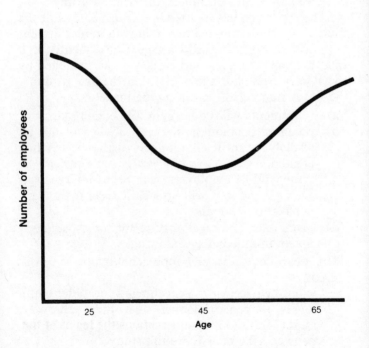

FIGURE 13
Analysing age distributions

organizations may well find this difficult at first but some attempt should be made to assess the implications for the future on what is being done in the present. Much of the work in the Civil Service sets out the basic principles.[7b]

It should be helpful to look at a practical example and list a few features and possible approaches to any problems that emerge. The age distribution in question is given in Figure 13 and represents the managerial employees of a marketing based engineering company.

The analysis of the organization need not concern us here, except to note that a period of expansion has followed an earlier decline in the firm's fortunes.

The expansion has resulted in recruitment, while the period of contraction led to a reduction in recruitment and probably to increased wastage. Consequently high numbers on young and old employees are matched by what may be a shortage of those in the age grouping 35-45. A number of points can be made:

(a) retirements will be heavy in the coming years
(b) potential promotions between 35-45 will not be available in sufficient numbers to fill the gaps thus created
(c) some young employees will probably received early promotions will attendant risks if they are not mature enough
(d) promotion blockages may result for those employees immdediately following.

What possible policies and approaches might be considered?,

(a) will it be necessary to encourage a few older employees to remain longer than they otherwise might? In this an other situations the terms of the pension scheme will require study
(b) if recruitment is taking place, can efforts be made to recruit 35-45 year olds?

(c)   if young people are to be promoted it is important that they have as much experience as possible, suggesting greater efforts towards planned career development in the next few years

(d)   loss of experience through retirement and replacements by younger employees will increase the importance of management development and training as ways of covering the loss in experience

(e)   if a promotion blockage results, ways of overcoming this such as changing current recruitment programmes or job rotation by lateral transfers might be considered.

Caution must be exercised as 'age discrimination', particularly in advertisements, may be limited by law as it is already in the USA. Still, with adequate analysis and thought the manager should be able to make good progress in understanding and solving these problems. A practical case study in reference (26) provides a fuller investigation, as does the excellent IMS literature (see Supplementary Reading List).

Promotions and transfers

The need for analysis of movements, such as wastage or recruitment, is more readily accepted than the analysis of promotions and transfers. This is partly because promotions and transfers are movements that occur, at least outwardly, solely at management's discretion. Assuming that promotion remains a motivator for employees, the manager will expect to improve or maintain retention and commitment by a properly managed promotion policy. Another reason for managing promotions is to meet the longer term succession needs of the organization by ensuring, for example, that potential managers are given the wide range of experience necessary.

Figure 14 shows a simple but effective way of indicat-

71

ing promotion patterns. Once future requirements have been identified it is not difficult to project this into the future and determine whether an increase or reduction in promotions is necessary. It is a matter of some argument whether it is true but it has been suggested (15) that past promotion rates encourage expectation in employees of what is likely to occur in the future. The argument continues that, if those expectations are not met, the effect will be increased wastage or reduced commitment and effort. In a contracting situation the organization may have the opportunity of balancing external recruitment and promotions from within, in that a greater reduction in recruitment may preserve promotion paths for current employees. This does not mean that this will be the best policy, though it indicates how a knowledge of past and present promotion practice may help the management of promotions and recruitment in the future. In any event decisions will be taken against a background of greater certainty as to likely consequences.

In promotion management, the manager is concerned with a number of aspects. The problem of promotion expectations of employees has already been mentioned. There are other considerations. An analysis of past promotion paths may show that a promotion policy has been adopted, such as recruiting management from the shop floor. Knowledge of the external environment will lead the manager to question how valid that would be in the future. It is possible that changing education patterns will result in the more able staying at school, and then receiving further education, rather than joining the firm on the shop floor. The manager must question whether past sources will be adequate in the future. He may have to face the political consequences of his findings. Craftsmen who lose a promotion path are unlikely to receive the change with

FIGURE 14
Promotion matrix

To
% moving to the category during year

	Manager	Deputy	Assistant	Super-intendent	Foreman	Manager Trainee
Manager	100					
Deputy	10	90				
Assistant	1	7	92			
Super-intendent			10	88	2	
Foreman				2	98	
Manager Trainee		1	6	11		82

%
From category during year

Notes: 1 The diagonal line represents the % *age of a category remaining in that category during the year*
2 *Therefore for assistant managers 92%* remain in post; 7% are promoted to deputy and 1% to manager

enthusiasm and may well refuse to be supervised or managed by other than trained and apprenticed craftsmen.

The manager is immediately considering how promotion policies lead to changes in other strategies, such as recruitment. It may be necessary to recruit from previously unused sources, such as colleges, universities or business schools to ensure that adequate promotion material exists. In practice, the manager will seek a balance between the various sources. Some promotions may continue from established channels (though fewer able people will still be available on the shop floor), some from college entrants, from young people trained in the firm and from mature recruits from the labour market.

Career and management development and succession planning

This activity implies that conscious attention is given to the problem of career development. If the organization does not extend its efforts in this way it will have to rely on filling all vacancies by *ad hoc* methods either from internal or external sources. The risks that the correct manpower will not be available or of waste of current managerial resources, with consequent effects on commitment and morale, are great.

How to manage careers is a difficult part of manpower planning. Expectations of employees seem to change and higher levels of education probably add to this difficulty. Career opportunity development is not an independent part of the organization's activity. Opportunities will be determined to a great extent by future manpower requirements. Management will have to consider the impact of the changes implied and balance recruitment and promotion in making career development decisions. A key decision to be taken is whether careers are expected to be within specialist areas, such as the professions or in departments or whether a more broadly based manager is required. This is a crucial decision.

The organization which wishes to limit the degree of chance in meeting future manpower levels will have to determine its promotion and career development rules. Though these are not always explicitly stated, if the manager analyses past practice he may well find that the firm operates a covert policy on, for example:

age on promotion to a certain grade or level
career development needs for certain positions
attributes required for certain positions, or
criteria on which future potential is judged.

Priority must be given to ensuring that the organization's immediate future needs are likely to be met. Over a relatively short period succession charts are often a useful device for highlighting problems of likely successors.

In Figure 15 there is a complete succession chart. Taking M S Purton, the first box (47) indicates his age; the second box (A) his present performance and the third box (A) his potential. The thicker rule surrounding his name shows that he is an immediate possible promotion, while Mr Dowes could do his job if Purton left. The ratings used in this example are in a scale ranging from A which stands for above average performance or high potential, to B which is average performance or potential, to C which is below average performance or potential. Normally these ratings can be drawn from appraisal interviews or from assessment centre reports where these are used. Although succession planning can highlight short term problems, the manager will be aware of the high degree of personal and subjective judgement involved in this process. The

FIGURE 15
Plans for succession

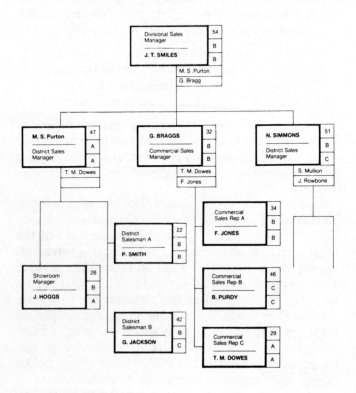

FIGURE 16
Earnings progression curves

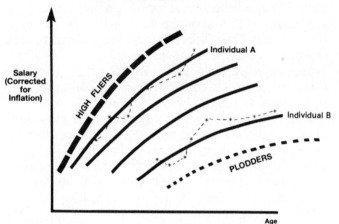

criteria on which such assessments are made require careful study. First, the manager should question whether a job in the current organization will be required in the future. Secondly, if so, the type of person required in the future needs consideration. It may be wrong to assume that current standards will prevail in the future. Thirdly, the criteria of assessing potential should be clearly stated. It would be wrong to rely on formal qualifications, though measured performance in the job may be more reliable. It should not need saying that 'heirs apparent' must be avoided at all costs.

There is no complete packaged method of identifying potential and it is probably necessary to work through the problems carefully. One method may be of value. This is based on Eliot Jacques' earnings progression curves. Jaques found that there was a useful relationship between age and salary when corrected for inflation and in fact the relationship was shown to follow a set pattern throughout a career. Figure 16 provides an example. The belief is that individuals tend to follow certain paths in their careers. Consequently it is possible to indicate future career development potential. An application of this method is described by Walmsley in reference (6). There are risks in this approach. It can be self-proving (high fliers are promoted quickly — which proves they are high fliers). But of course the more subjective methods currently used in many organizations are not without similar problems.

It can be seen that we are referring to the manpower theme mentioned in chapter 1. The theme can be used in respect of planning for managers as shown in Figure 17(a). Again policy and operations are not in conflict but rather means to the end of planning managerial careers for individuals in organizations. If we are concerned with operations then the decisions are of the 'which person' nature. Here we are concerned with recruiting to fill a particular post or selecting a manager for a managerial course and so on. This can be called succession planning. On the other hand longer term questions are raised by career development. Here the question is 'what kind of person is required?' This is manpower planning proper. This is the problem that must be answered first and which is often avoided.

The idea that careers can be managed does not come easily. New ways of looking at careers have been developed. Called the career progression diagram, it was developed by A. R. Smith and his colleagues at the Civil Service Department. An example of a typical diagram is given in Figure 17(b). The diagram is easily obtained. It is only necessary to know the total number of employees in each grade by age. (The grades can of course be occupations, levels of management and so on — they are titled grades I to IV here for convenience.) The graph is drawn by working out the percentage of each age grouping in each grade. Various points can

FIGURE 17(a)
Planning for managers

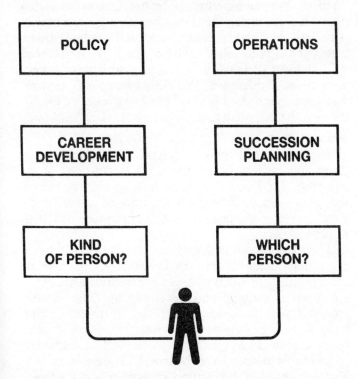

then be considered. In Figure 17(b) for instance it can be seen that few managers, up to their late 20s have been promoted into grade II, while the number quickly increases in the early 30s. Those who are not promoted out of grade I by the age of 40 will only get to grade II at the most. It is possible to develop this theme as shown in Figure 17(c). In this figure 'streams' have been drawn, the implication being that those managers who are promoted early to grade II similarly are promoted early to grades III and IV. Taken in conjunction with management development and appraisal information it may be possible to remove some of the chance element in identifying management potential. One suspects that there is a great deal here that has hardly been understood at the present time. Interested readers should study the full published Civil Service work (which after all has been successfully managing careers for a very long time) in reference 7(b). Only a sample of its work has been touched on here. (See also references 49, 50, 57 and the Supplementary Reading List.)

Recruitment

One object of the supply analysis and forecast will be to determine current future needs for recruitment programmes. Many jobs now call for lengthy training before full effectiveness is reached and this so-called 'lead-time' increases the need to recruit in advance of actual requirements.

The manager has to decide how much he will rely on recruiting 'ready made' employees from the labour market and how much he expects to recruit employees for internal training and development. The former approach will be cheaper and easier (if it works); the latter is more expensive but carries with it greater certainty that the right type of employee will be available. In practice a balance has to be struck. The manager will bear in mind the likely supply of particular skills from the labour market. He will also concentrate on areas crucial to his operation when considering internal training and development.

Recruitment presents a major opportunity to change the nature and structure of the labour force. Over a period, it becomes possible to increase, say, the managerial potential available or the supply of skilled employees. The age distribution problem shown in Figure 13 might have been alleviated by recruiting employees to create a better balance.

FIGURE 17(b)
Career progression diagram

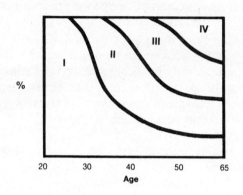

FIGURE 17(c)
Prospectus

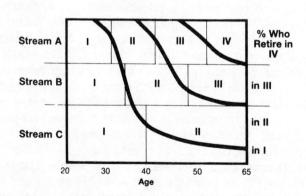

NB The vertical lines are the average age of promotion to the next grade.

External manpower environment

A key feature affecting internal recruitment policies (and indeed all manpower policies) will be the forces exerted from the external manpower environment. The manager will be concerned with:

local supply of manpower by skill

local and regional unemployment trends

economic activity by local firms and at national level

activity of competitors or other firms (especially where expansion or contraction is involved)

total local and national labour force

education trends

social trends (such as extension of opportunities for women)

unemployment and short time.

Trends in education may be more important than may be supposed though the effects may take longer to work through. Obvious examples that require careful study are the numbers and changing trends in the supply of young people. The organization will need to assess how a rise or fall in the school leaving age will affect its policies both in the year it occurs and subsequently, because there may be longer term effects. Inseparable from this will be the supply of young people from the education system at higher levels, such as at 18+ or from universities and colleges. Figure 18(a) shows the increased stock of highly qualified manpower between 1981 and 1988 (forecast). Such a major change cannot take place without having a major effect on organizational employment policies. Obvious examples are the increasing shortage of able employees available for employment at 16 (such as through apprenticeships), and the increasing numbers of young people who are educationally and socially sophisticated.

Government legislation and social trends have an occasional if dramatic effect on manpower policies.

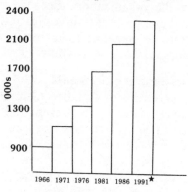

FIGURE 18(a)
Stock of highly qualified manpower 1966-91

* Forecast

Numbers are degree or equivalent

Legislation on racial discrimination, equal pay, opportunities for women or the Industrial Training Act are examples. There is as yet no clearly co-ordinated national strategy for manpower, although the Manpower Services Commission, set up in 1974, is committed to filling this need. Though its practical use to a manager planning manpower in most industrial environments is small at the moment it will presumably develop.

The dearth of good manpower information both nationally and locally will probably be the manager's major current problem. Again, there have been indications of a change (see for instance references 37, 58 and especially 65), but for the moment he must make do with what is available and will frequently find himself having to forecast the past because of the delays in publishing information. A few texts which should be of practical value are given in the references and the interested manager might also find it useful to contact local and regional employment offices.

83

One final point should be made: a great deal of the investigation of the external environment may depend on action by the organization. Because it may also demand special and prolonged investigation, it is often useful to nominate someone to maintain a watching brief for the organization as a whole.

Analysis of training requirements

Training provides a major and direct source of supply on new employees, both in the present and the future. Except where someone is recruited for training directly from outside, the 'newness' relates to a qualitative change following the acquisition of new skills.

The knowledge gained from manpower planning will be a direct input to training activity and should indicate the employees to be trained by occupation both in the present and in the future. Obviously these intentions should be subject to constant review, though good planning should ensure that few problems should arise that cannot be adequately solved. The flexibility that this implies means that the training manager must be fully involved in the planning process and must make his own contribution.

Redundancy

If the purported overmanning and inefficiency in industry is true, it is hardly surprising that a complete analysis of needs often leads to the identification of surplus manpower.

Regrettably, redundancy will occasionally be seen as a possible method of affecting the supply of manpower. If planning is effective at least the worst excesses of sudden redundancies should be avoided. It should be possible to identify surpluses in advance so that the impact can be lessened, wastage allowed to take some effect and employees given time to consider their position. A good redundancy scheme should be developed which gives at least a level of financial compensation. The manager's knowledge of the labour market and his relationships with outside bodies and other firms should help him to know what the market is for his surplus employees. The planning of manpower strategies will mean that recruitment is not taking place unnecessarily, while analysis of training available and development opportunities will highlight possibilities for retraining employees for other work in the organization. Finally, the integration of manpower into business policy may increase the feasibility of the organization looking at ways of expanding its markets. Often a manpower surplus is seen as a millstone when it might usefully be looked on as an opportunity for development in new markets.

Sickness and absenteeism—'withdrawal from work' concept

Although accurate information is not always available nor its significance fully recognized, many organizations are aware of the need to look at factors which result in employees not attending work. Various aspects of absence are: holidays with pay, holidays without pay, absenteeism absence (absence usually certified, resulting from sickness), unofficial disputes, official disputes (including strikes, work to rule etc), lateness and general bad time keeping, accidents, wastage.

More direct indicators of poor morale and commitment such as low productivity, sub-standard workmanship or poor customer service are increasingly being related to absence. The total losses due to all these causes are substantial and in certain industries some reach chronic proportions. They have generally been regarded as isolated factors but, as knowledge of human behaviour has advanced, greater understanding of them has been reached.

Among the many studies undertaken, a famous one was carried out at a large chemical plant. The company employed psychologists because of an increasing and worrying rise in accidents at the plant. The decision to call in psychologists was itself interesting as it recognized the failure of existing approaches. The resulting study showed that a large number of days lost through accidents were attributable to a small proportion of the labour force, who tended to have repeated separate absences. After discussion with the employees, they were moved to jobs in office conditions where the prospect of accidents was small. The effect was intended: the accident rate quickly reduced. To the surprise of managers it was not long before sickness absence began to increase and was found to be attributable to a few employees — those who only a few months before had experienced a series of accidents.

A similar effect was found by Elton Mayo in his well-known studies of Hawthorne Electric Company where, as employees became more involved in the work being undertaken, stability increased and sickness and absenteeism declined.

Another more practical example is given by Johnston in reference (43). The diagram in Figure 18(b) is reproduced from the published report. It shows that the diseases that strike employees down are more active on Mondays and Fridays and are considerably less powerful on Thursdays. For those weekly paid employees the reader may not need to be told that Thursday is pay day! For shift workers whose week starts and finishes on Saturdays and Sundays those same diseases are more effective on those days.

The implications of such observations have been reaffirmed many times and a number of firms find that increases in absenteeism run concurrently with strikes, falls in productivity and increasing wastage.

FIGURE 18(b)
Sickness

Start day – SHIFT WORKERS

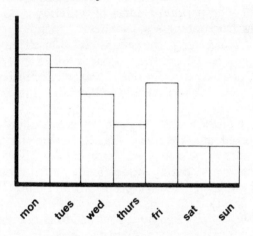

Start days – ALL WORKERS

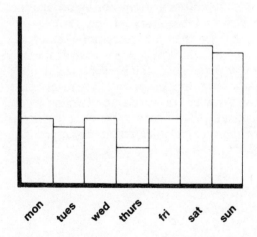

A body of knowledge is therefore developing which regards disputes, sickness, absenteeism etc., not as isolated but as inter-dependent phenomena, using the argument that they are various forms by which the employee is able to avoid the conflict and pressures in his job. The particular form of withdrawal adopted, varying from lateness to sickness, depends on many factors concerning the employee himself and the organization. Often they occur simultaneously but sometimes an increase in one is associated with a decline in another. This is discussed in more detail in Bryant's work.[16]

The manager must be cautious in his approach to such problems, for they suggest manifestations of deep-rooted human problems that are poorly researched and hardly understood, and it would be wrong to deal with the symptoms without some effort to handle the cause.

Unfortunately, the cause may well be at the centre of how industrial society has developed and is organized. Because of this many people accept strikes as having a functional value in working out the frustrations and tensions which often arise in boring occupations. The manager should be aware of the various aspects of absence and see them as indicators of emerging problems, and ones which may be easier to deal with in their early stages. In any event, if he wishes to identify future manpower requirements he will have to take such losses into account when determining manning levels.

The final aspect of manpower supply to consider is the leaving process, which will be discussed in the next chapter.

5 Analysing manpower supply—II

Wastage analysis
Wastage analysis has received widespread attention for a number of reasons. First, data for wastage analysis has been available and statisticians have been able to use techniques developed in other fields.

A second reason for analysing wastage is the important effect it has on the organization. It is not difficult to find examples of entire recruitment, training, promotion and development strategies within firms which are dependent on people leaving. In this situation an analysis of wastage patterns is an important first step in manpower planning: without it effective manpower strategies for recruitment, training and promotion are impossible to achieve. An example illustrates the importance of wastage to other manpower policies. It is not uncommon for management to become involved in annual rituals concerning recruitment of a given category and much effort and argument may be expended in determining whether to recruit 80 or 90 apprentices or 15 or 20 graduates. Such decisions are important but they should be seen in their proper context. The real determinant may not be the recruitment level but the present and future rate of wastage. Consequently management should have a better understanding of manpower by concentrating less on marginal recruitment decisions and more on understanding the leaving process.

A distinction should be made between wastage and labour turnover. Wastage is an element of labour turnover. Wastage is a severance but is not turnover unless a replacement is made: for example, redundancy is wastage but not labour turnover. Labour turnover thus embraces recruitment, wastage and promotions.

This book tends to use the less ambitious term 'wastage' rather than 'labour turnover'. Wastage includes all severances. Most of the so-called measures of labour turnover are in practice only measures of wastage (severance), in which no effort is usually made to include the whole leaving and replacement process (turnover).

For the purpose of this chapter, wastage is considered as a severance from the organization and includes voluntary resignations, retirements, deaths and dismissals. This excludes promotions or transfers from one department to another. Certainly they are different processes, though possibly with related causes, but the manager who experiences the loss caused by someone promoting his employees may find the difference academic. It is sensible to separate wastage and promotions for purposes of measurement but in practice one cannot be analysed to the exclusion of the other.

Review of wastage

Much early work took the form of a series of studies at the Glacier Metal Company, as part of the Glacier Project by social scientists of the Tavistock Institute of Human Relations. The idea of wastage as a social process emerged, also the early development of statistical work. This work is reported in references (27) and (30) from which much of this chapter has been drawn.

An important point among those emerging from

FIGURE 19
Wastage as a semi-stable process

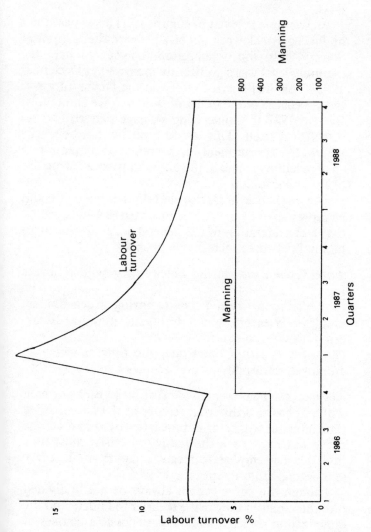

these studies was that wastage was a quasi-stationary (semi-stable) process, which if disturbed (by, say, recruitment) would eventually revert to a previous level.

An example is given in Figure 19. This is based not on the Tavistock work but on a paper to the Manpower Society.[36] In the organization represented here the manning level was significantly increased in December 1986. This had a sharp effect on the labour turnover index because of the influx of short service employees. By late 1987 the underlying wastage pattern had re-established itself. This would probably not hold true where the recruitment programme or organization change led to change in the underlying social structure of the organization.

The Tavistock work also showed that wastage could be represented by the curve illustrated in Figure 20 and that a consideration of the general shape of the curve highlighted three identifiable phases:

the induction crisis, during which 'marginal' employees leave
the period of differential transit, during which time an employee is learning about the organization and discovering his own role in it
the period of settled connection, the time at which an employee settles down and becomes a long stayer.

The data can be presented in many ways, each of which will emphasize a different feature of the curve. Long time intervals will bring out the latter two phases of the curve but may mask the induction crisis; short time intervals may emphasize irregular patterns in the curve and detract from its meaning.

Though the curve cannot always be neatly divided into these phases they make it easier to understand the organization patterns and suggest possible courses of

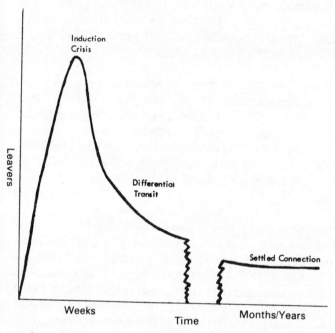

FIGURE 20
Wastage curves showing patterns of leaving

action. For instance, if excess wastage existed among short stayers, a different solution would be needed that if long stayers were leaving. No absolute time periods are associated with each phase, which is largely dependent on the type of job being considered; for example the induction crisis could vary from a few weeks for a labourer to a few months for a graduate.

These studies brought out the importance of the relationship between leaving and length of service and the ability to express that relationship as a standard mathematical curve. The use of this measurement and forecasting will be discussed below.

Characteristics of wastage

A degree of understanding valuable to the manager who wishes to get to grips wtih the wastage problem has emerged from the various studies of wastage. The main characteristics are discussed in the following paragraphs (these are expanded on with further references in references (27), (30) and (32)):

Wastage decreases as length of service increases
This characteristic is so important and so well documented that its mathematical aspects approach the status of a natural law. This relationship with tenure is the basis of most methods of forecasting wastage. Most cases show a rise in the early period of service followed by the fall which results in the familiar curve shown in Figure 20.

Wastage is higher among females than males
The Glacier studies and others support this, though it is possible that changing social patterns will affect its importance. It is known that where women are given similar opportunities to men, their stability patterns are similar to men. With the use of maternity provisions, this also applies to women of child-bearing age.

Wastage decreases as skill exercised increases
Inadequate definitions of skill make this proposition difficult to prove. It can be shown that the skilled craftsman leaves at a rate lower than that of the unskilled labourer, and the manager at a rate lower than that of the skilled craftsman, suggesting that wastage decreases as skill exercised increases. There are contrary examples. For instance wastage of computer programmers has for many firms been very high, an example presumably where market forces counter normal expectations.

It is possible that part of the problem is not that the job itself is causing wastage but that less status is attached to some jobs than to others. The consequent lack of 'job-satisfaction' through insufficient recognition of status would be expected to increase wastage.

In any event in a position where less skill is exercised it takes less time to understand the nature of the duties and the employee would, therefore, be able to determine sooner whether he wished to continue to do them. This would also result in increased wastage.

Finally, where firms promote from lower to higher skilled jobs from their own employees, the wastage rate for the lower skilled would be higher because there would be more employees with shorter service in the group.

Consequently, when making comparisons such as these, it is important to ensure that like is compared with like on length of service; thus that for any given length of service group wastage would be expected to decrease as skill and status rose.

Wastage rates vary with the level of employment
Many studies support this. An example of the effect is illustrated in Figure 21, which suggests a significant relationship between wastage and unemployment. This relationship has been found to hold good more for unskilled manual than clerical or professional workers and is less true for women. This is probably partly due to the make-up of the unemployed force rather than to anything inherent in the jobs themselves. Increased benefits protect people more from the worst effects of unemployment and so it may be less feared than it was.

The manager should find it possible to graph the relationship of unemployment to leaving in certain occupations and have a good idea how many will leave (or stay) as unemployment falls (or rises). However the

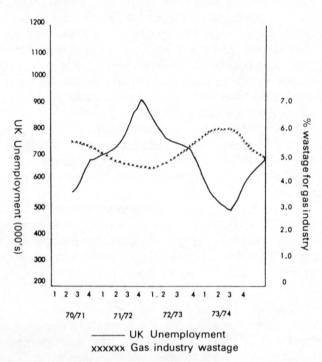

FIGURE 21
UK unemployment and gas industry wastage

——— UK Unemployment
xxxxxx Gas industry wastage

effect and existence of continued high rates of unemployment will need to be considered.

Wastage exhibits seasonal variations
As a rule December wastage is low and January's high, while peaks in spring and autumn are separated by a trough in the summer. One problem is that troughs occur at holiday periods and it seems possible that wastage reduces, simply because of holidays. There is simply less opportunity to leave at holiday times, the month being thereby effectively shortened. These pat-
96

terns may differ with certain firms and an analysis of individual wastage patterns by weeks throughout the year is required, with holiday weeks highlighted.

Wastage declines as age increases
It is difficult to separate increasing age from increasing length of service, though there is evidence that age may be a separate, if minor contributory factor.

There are other characteristics of wastage on which the evidence is fragmentary.

Employees are attracted from lower to higher paid occupations
Intuitively this would be expected to be so. A difficulty in proving it arises because a change to a higher paid job often means promotion. Consequently it is the promotion and not just the higher paid occupation which is attracting the employee. To avoid this problem it would be necessary to analyse the attidudes of employees leaving one job to go to the same job elsewhere.

Recent evidence seeks to re-assert the importance of orthodox economic theory, which social scientists have tended to play down in relation to wastage. A problem is that to the surprise of employers the employee is often not aware what competitive rates are and therefore cannot be attracted by them. The problem for the firm is why the employee begins to look for a new job in the first place.

Wastage depends on the size of the firm
The large 'impersonal' firm might be expected to have difficulty in retaining its employees compared with the smaller firm, but evidence is conflicting.

Wastage depends on working conditions
This is to be expected but it is difficult to prove, little

information being available.

It will be noticed that these points refer to 'characteristics' rather than 'causes' of wastage. Knowing that wastage is related to length of service may facilitate forecasting but it does not say why people leave. A person does not leave because he has a short length of service: rather, the factors that will push an individual into leaving have more effect on short serving employees whose bond with the firm is less strong.

Long serving employees may be so tied by pension schemes that leaving is not possible without considerable financial loss, though pension scheme revisions will lessen this effect.

No clear link has ever been shown between 'job satisfaction' and wastage. The early search for job satisfaction has moved its focus from the 'job' to the 'firm' itself. This is the motivation shown in the flexible firm and the 'excellent' companies (see Supplementary Reading List).

Methods of analysing wastage

The labour turnover index

This index is basically the number of leavers expressed as a percentage of average employees. It is often referred to as the BIM index (it was proposed in a British Institute Management booklet in 1949) and also as the 'crude' turnover (or wastage) index. Much has been written about it, though there is still a widespread ignorance as to what a meaningless statistic it can be, in certain circumstances for the purpose of helping a manager to make decisions.

Basically the index is derived as follows:

$$\frac{Labour}{turnover} = \frac{Number\ leaving\ in\ a\ period}{Average\ number\ employed\ in\ the\ period} \times 100$$

The average number employed is usually achieved by adding the employees at the start and end of the period and dividing by two. This should be sufficiently accurate unless the number employed vary considerably over the period. One year is usually the period to which the index refers, but any period can be used as long as the period is made clear when comparison of indices is intended. It is often a good idea to produce a moving annual index. This entails recalculating the index each month (or quarter) for the previous 12 months, and then plotting the points obtained. In this way it is possible to draw a graph and see how the annual index is moving.

FIGURE 22
Example of labour turnover index

This is defined as

$$\frac{\text{Number of men leaving in a period}}{\text{Average number employed in that period}} \times 100$$

(i) At the start of a year a firm has 110 employees; at the end of the year it has 90. No recruitment is made.

Number leaving $= 110 - 90 = 20$

$$\text{Average number employed} = \frac{110 + 90}{2}$$
$$= 100$$

Labour turnover $= \frac{20}{100} \times 100 = \underline{\underline{20\%}}$

(ii) Suppose that 10 men had been recruited during the year and the number at start and finish are as example (i) then:

Number leaving $= 110 + 10 - 90 = 30$
Average number employed $= 100$
Labour turnover $= \underline{\underline{30\%}}$

The example of calculating the index in Figure 22 will be helpful. It shows the simple calculation of the index for one period (in this case a year).

The weakness of the basic turnover index has been demonstrated for some time.

The following example is taken from a much quoted paper by two statisticians, Lane and Andrew.[31] After studying a steel company they came up with the example shown in Figure 23.

FIGURE 23
Labour turnover

Department	A.1	A.2
Average employed	1,117	382
Leavers	98	65
Index of turnover (wastage)	8.8%	17.3%
Expectation of service	5 yrs	7 yrs

Using the standard index it would seem that department A.1 was considerably more stable than department A.2. On closer analysis it transpired that an individual's expectation of service in A.1 was five years and in A.2 was seven years; that is, A.1 was less stable than A.2, which conflicted with what was expected in view of the standard index of turnover. Why was there this discrepancy?

As mentioned earlier an important factor affecting wastage is the length of service of an individual; that is, the probability of leaving decreases as service increases. The discrepancy between the two measures was due to department A.2 having gone through a period of rapid expansion bringing in a large number of new staff. This meant that the length of service distribution had been pulled sharply to the lower end — and it is the people at that lower end who are most likely to leave. Therefore this crude labour turnover index gave what could be regarded as a misleading picture of the wastage pattern of the two departments. The importance of this to manpower planning is that what is needed is a measure which can predict future wastage and take into account both staying and leaving characteristics. In an effort to provide a prediction of wastage for use with manpower planning, the labour turnover index, being so unstable and reflecting changes in length of service, may be little short of useless.

To interpret and understand wastage the manager must also look at length of service distributions of the groups of employees he is considering. In situations of rapid recruitment and curtailment of recruitment, the index, reflecting changes in the length of service distribution, can give misleading indications of the stability of the firm's manpower.

The same index can be achieved by entirely different wastage patterns as shown in Figure 24 and this is another weakness.

In Figure 24 the represented organization has 10 employees, each leaves and is replaced (10 leavers) and the wastage is 100 per cent as shown in example A. If nine employees remain and one employee leaves and is replaced 10 times (10 leavers) the wastage index is still 100 per cent as shown in example B. The problem to the firm is probably completely different. In the first example a widespread problem affecting all jobs is suggested while in the second most employees are not affected but the firm is having difficulty retaining its new recruits. In the first case a fundamental review of the organization may be necessary, while in the second

FIGURE 24
Same wastage index from different wastage patterns

Example A

Employees	= 10
Nine leave and are replaced	
Leavers	= 9
Wastage index	= 90%

Example B

Employees	= 10
One leaves and is replaced 9 times	
Leavers	= 9
Wastage index	= 90%

it may only be recruitment or induction methods that are at fault, and the problem might easily be dealt with.

Before leaving the index it should be noted that criticism of it may have been overdone. In its defence, it is easy to compute and, given a stable labour force, it can be useful especially in aggregated forms.

It is better to know the percentage of leavers than nothing else. It would not be surprising to see the index regaining a measure of respectability, calculated according to length of service — say excluding all employees with less than one year's service. But it must be recognized that, if the age and recruitment history of groups are dissimilar, the index can be misleading. Few organizations these days will have the degree of stability in age, recruitment and length of service distributions to make the index a reliable indicator of present or future wastage patterns.

The stability index
In an attempt to overcome this problem the stability index[28] was proposed which attempts to distinguish

between the wastage patterns given above; that is, where all jobs are turning over or where a few jobs are turning over rapidly. The stability index is defined as:

$$\frac{\text{Number with more than 1 year's service now}}{\text{Total employed 1 year ago}} \times 100$$

An example using it is given in Figure 25.

FIGURE 25

Department A 10 employees of which 9 leave and are replaced a) Standard turnover index=90% b) Stability index $\dfrac{1 \times 100}{10}$ = 10%	*Department B* 10 employees of which one leaves and is replaced 9 times a) Standard turnover index=90% b) Stability index $\dfrac{9 \times 100}{10}$ = 90%

In this example the two departments have two different wastage patterns but the standard turnover index is the same in both cases. In department A the underlying problem is revealed in the low stability index, drawing management's attention to the problem. In department B the general health is shown by the high stability (90 per cent) and management's attention is drawn to the problem of retaining new recruits. It is also possible to calculate 'skill dilution' and 'skill wastage' indices and these can be studied in the references at the end of this book.

Cohort analysis

While indices such as the standard labour turnover (wastage) index or the stability index are useful guides for manpower planning on the state of health of a firm, a

103

more precise tool capable of use in forecasting is required. It has already been noted that one of the key characterstics of wastage is its relationship to length of service. The weakness of the standard labour turnover index is its failure to take into account the length of service variable. Methods are available for the manager which both demonstrate and allow him to use the relationship of wastage and length of service especially in forecasting wastage. One such method is cohort analysis (in this context cohort means a homogeneous group). This requires following the wastage (or rate of survival) of a group (cohort) of employees through time. The group should be as similar as possible in terms of personal employee characteristics, occupation and time of recruitment.

In practice smallness of groups will lead to aggregating, with a consequent effect on the reliability of forecasts. A further problem is that the forecast assumes that time is a constant: that is, what occurred in the past will occur in the future. Changing social and economic conditions could invalidate this. While the practical applications on a wide scale may be few, experience in using the method is essential for understanding wastage analysis.

An example of the cohort analysis method will be helpful. Figure 26(a) relates to a group of employees recruited to the same occupation over three months, making them sufficiently homogeneous. Figure 26(a) follows their wastage pattern. After one month 46 had left so that 90.6 per cent of the original group remained. After two months an additional 37 had left leaving only 83.1 per cent of the original group and so on.

The percentage remaining can be presented on graph paper; it is known as a survival curve because it shows the percentage of employees surviving (and remaining) at different points in time. This is derived by:

$$\frac{number\ remaining\ at\ a\ given\ time}{number\ engaged\ at\ start} \times 100$$

It is useful to plot each point shown in column 5 of Figure 26(a) on graph paper resulting in the curve shown in Figure 26(b).

FIGURE 26(a)
Cohort analysis

Number engaged = 491

(1) Length of Service (months)	(2) Number Leaving	(3) Cumulative Leavers	(4) Remaining	(5) (Survival curve) (%) Remaining
0	0	0	491	100.0
1	46	46	445	90.6
2	37	83	408	83.1
3	23	106	385	78.4
4	25	131	360	73.3
5	19	150	341	69.5
6	12	162	329	67.0
7	13	175	316	64.4
8	7	182	309	62.9
9	8	190	301	61.3
10	2	192	299	60.9
11	9	201	290	59.1
12	7	208	283	57.6
13	4	212	279	56.8
14	3	215	276	56.2
15	6	221	270	55.0
16	1	222	269	54.8
17	2	224	268	54.4
18	6	230	263	53.2

The resulting curve is shown in Figure 26(b)

It will be noticed that the curve is similar to that shown in Figure 20. This is because both relate leaving to length of service and as service increases there is a tendency for stability to increase. A feature of the wastage pattern shown in Figure 26(b) is that, when the curve is plotted on a particular sort of graph paper known as 'log-probability' paper, the curve becomes a straight line (see Figure 26(c)). In effect the straightness of the line (mathematically it is referred to as a 'curve') indicates the degree of relationship between wastage

105

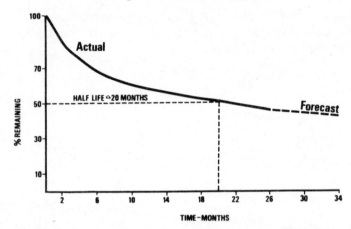

FIGURE 26(b)
Wastage curve (cohort analysis)

and length of service. In the example shown the points are relatively close to the line, suggesting a good relationship.

This has the advantage that the line can be extended into the future and thus a prediction of future wastage obtained. In the example in Figure 26(c) the dotted line indicates the projection into the future. This shows that, assuming the relationship continues, the initial stock of some 490 which had reduced to 329 after six months would become 283 within a year. This sort of analysis gives a manager information on future manning levels and can be used in a variety of ways, such as for budget purposes to indicate future costs or to ascertain recruitment and training needs.

Another useful concept emerges from Figure 26(c), that of the 'half-life', usually attributed to D T Bryant.[20] This term equates with its use in relation to radiation in that the half-life of a group (or cohort) is the time it takes for half of the original group to waste. Its usefulness is twofold: it provides a measure of stability

FIGURE 26(c)
Wastage curve plotted from log graph paper

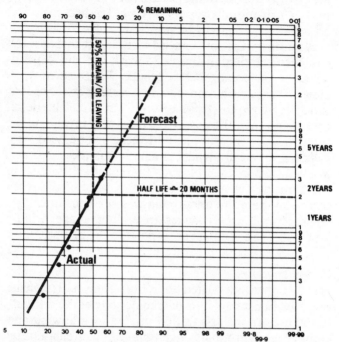

that can be related to other jobs and firms because it is independent of length of service: in other words firms or departments can compare half-lives to indicate real differences in wastage and not those resulting from recent recruitment; secondly, it can be used as a guide to recruitment. For instance, if 10 graduates at a certain level were required in four years' time and the half-life of graduates is four years, 29 would need to be recruited now. The half-life of a group can be determined easily by cohort analysis as indicated in Figure 26(c). In this example the half-life is about 20 months.

Half-lives vary with occupation. A relatively volatile

group such as labourers may have a half-life of a few months (such as the example given here) whereas a group of graduates in the gas industry has been found to have a half-life of over four years. In career services half-lives are likely to be much larger.

A number of problems arise with cohort analysis. It is cumbersome though simple to work out and depends on having a homogeneous group. Where turnover is slow (as, say, with managers in a career service) a long time may have to elapse before a curve can be determined and then the passage of time may invalidate the forecast. The measure should therefore be used with caution, especially where dramatic changes such as a marked shift in unemployment levels or contraction in the firm may change the social structure of the work force and therefore underlying wastage behaviour patterns. Even if such changes arise, the manager will be better able to anticipate or respond to the new situation if he has a reliable measure of wastage.

Census analysis
Another method related to cohort analysis is census analysis. Census analysis overcomes one of the difficulties of cohort analysis in that instead of following one homogeneous group through time (when often no sufficiently homogeneous groups exist) the method involves taking a census or 'snapshot' of the total situation. Three sets of data are required:

1 the number of employees at the start of the census
2 the number of employees at the end of the census
3 the number of leavers during the census period.

In each case the length of service must be known. It is also necessary to specify the time period of the census which is usually, though not necessarily, a year.

The method gives what is referred to as a stability curve and is similar in shape to that obtained by the
108

cohort method shown in Figure 26(b). This is not surprising as in effect a number of cohorts are being considered at one time. One advantage is that data is more readily available for whole groups in employment at one time rather than for groups recruited at a particular time; since it is not necessary to follow a group through time the method is less cumbersome. Another advantage is that using only recent data will probably make it more accurate as the environment changes less over shorter periods.

Using this method it is possible to calculate the probability of leaving of recruits and present employees; consequently a forecast of future manning levels can be obtained as well as determining a recruitment programme. The full mathematics which are not unduly difficult are given in a number of sources, for example (7a) and (3).

Wastage profiles
It is probably appropriate to suggest a method of wastage analysis that can be reliable, simple to use and simple to understand. This is particularly important where adequate statistical skills are not readily available to the manager or where the personnel manager either wishes to use the method himself or explain it and make use of it with another manager. It has been noted that the standard index of labour turnover is unreliable because of its failure to account for changes in the length of service distribution of employees. It is proposed that the standard index be used but that it be broken down by length of service groupings, as shown in Figure 27. It is also possible to use this method as a forecast of future retention. This can be estimated mathematically or the manager can make his own estimates of wastage after allowing for changes in unemployment levels and other factors. The information

needed is employees by length of service groupings. Leavers can then be expressed as a percentage of this figure.

Such a method avoids the worst features of the standard index (that is, not taking variations in service into account) without involving complex mathematical calculations. The length of service groupings necessary must be determined by experience and will probably vary between categories of employee. The manager who requires a simple index may try separating employees between those with less than one year's service

FIGURE 27
Wastage index by length of service

	Average employed	Leavers	% Wastage	% Wastage by length of service—months			
				0-6	6-12	13-24	25+
Managers	10	2	20	100	—	—	—
Salesmen	105	17	16	64	30	16	—
Clerks	10	6	60	80	—	—	—

NB 1 This shows that % wastage is greater in earlier months of service.
　　 2 The forecast depends on the numbers in each service group and this must be estimated by looking at progression and recruitment.
　　 3 Where employees transfer from another part of the organization or from an affiliated firm it is sensible to carry their length of service with them and not count them as having no service.

and those with more as this at least removes the risk of high wastage rates in early periods of service affecting the overall wastage rate.

Such a simple method must be used with caution and, as the need for accuracy grows, more complex statistical methods using computers will probably be necessary. In the meantime the attempt to account for variations in length of service given here will probably facilitate improvement both in terms of analysis and forecasting.

Reasons for leaving and exit interviews

Earlier in this chapter reference was made to the poor state of knowledge of the underlying behavioural causes of an employee leaving. A favourite scapegoat is often money and certainly employees will leave to go where they can get more. Despite repeated failures to find a satisfactory explanation as to why people really leave there are still many organizations who place inordinate faith in the exit interview. Perhaps when undertaken in depth, extensively, systematically and with trained interviewers, it may be possible to unearth the variety of complex factors underlying human behaviour. Unfortunately, many exit interviews consist of untrained staff asking simple questions of the 'low pay', 'did not like the boss' type. Apart from the difficulty of identifying such reasons (even the employee may be unsure of his true motives) they are anyway not discrete. The decision to leave may not be caused by any one factor but by a combination of a variety. It would be more useful in general practice to rely on more objective reasons as shown in Figure 28 and to reserve the behavioural analyses for special problem areas when trained behavioural scientists can be employed to undertake the study.

FIGURE 28
Reasons for leaving employment

Code	Classification	Reasons for leaving (details)	Code
01	Retirement	Normal	02
		Early	03
		Ill-health	04
06	Redundancy		
08	Discharge	Unsuitable	09
		Disciplinary	10
12	Death		
15	Transfer	To other region	16
		To headquarters	17
20	Voluntary	Marriage	21
	Resignation	Pregnancy	22
		Ill-health	23
		Left district (incl. emigration)	24
		Other—better pay, prospects, conditions, etc	25
		Full-time study	26

6 Formulating flexible manpower plans

Planning is concerned with change and with achieving objectives which themselves change. It implies an ability (and a desire) to select an alternative and work towards it. The forecasting of supply and demand and the analysis of the present environment are an integral part of the planning process. Forecasts are passive views of what the future holds in store, flexible plans are dynamic intentions of where the organization wishes to be with tactics of how it expects to get there. If the hopes and expectations in forecasting are not purposively carried through into planning, the manager and the organization will not achieve the changes hoped for. These changes can be identified at three levels:

    strategic changes
    policy changes
    operational changes.

Strategic change is concerned with long term manoeuvring with resources. Policy changes will spring from overall strategic decisions and will be concerned with putting policy flesh onto the bones of strategy. Operational change is the planning which will primarily be the concern of the line manager. The concern is with putting policy decisions into practice.

Strategic change will be the responsibility of the board or other overall controlling authority, because some manpower planning needs to be undertaken at the level of the entire organization. A major change in the environment, such as increasing numbers of qualified manpower, may force a change to which all departments must agree.

Career planning and management development may well be dealt with at the strategy level, where individuals might more sensibly be regarded as an organizational rather than a departmental resource. Policy decisions may well be the responsibility of the board. An example might be how its strategic aim of management career planning is to be brought about. Policy decisions may also be taken one level down at the managing divisional/functional level.

The line manager will try to meet the organization's objectives. This will often involve him in undertaking activities which are not in his own department's interests but will serve the interests of the organization as a whole. If the manpower plans are to be implemented, it is essential to ensure that the line manager understands his objectives and knows why they have come about. The methods used and the criteria and reasons for success must be understood. If a 'backroom' exercise has taken place, management at all levels will have limited, if any, commitment and failure to achieve change will be inevitable.

The manpower planning cycle
It may be helpful to present this relationship in terms of the diagram shown in Figure 29. The hierarchy of planning decisions affects divisions/functions and finally operating departments. The purpose is to link short and long range planning; consequently budgets are shown as part of the cycle. Many organizations, espe-

FIGURE 29
Manpower planning cycle

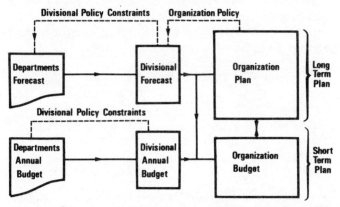

cially larger ones, will have an explicit cycle in some ways similar to that shown here; in small organizations such a cycle may be more informal. Budgeting must not be a separate financial exercise. Without wishing to disturb the important financial management of the organization, benefit accrues where the budget became part of the organization's planning procedure, because the planning cycle is concerned with the achievement of the organization's objectives through the decision making process.

Apart from linking long and short term planning the cycle has two major purposes:

to ensure that departmental and organizational plans are not in conflict, that they are coherent,
to ensure that plans are implemented.

Forming integrated plans
The manpower planning process described in chapter 2 is referred to again here. The purpose of the planning stage is to ensure that the organization's plans are integrated to such an extent that no one is in conflict with the

115

direction being taken by another. In simple terms, this means that one department should not be carrying surplus manpower while another is short and as a result is having difficulty meeting its objectives. The organization will be concerned with forming integrated and flexible plans for all personnel activities, such as:

recruitment	retirement
redeployment	contractors
retraining	career planning
overtime	industrial relations
management development	promotion
redundancy	training
remuneration	accommodation

The object of a planning cycle should be not only to remove areas of conflict but also to activate the organization in such a way that mutual support sharpens effectiveness. Integration of and commitment to plans implies understanding and probably involvement. It is worth considering the roles of various departmental managers in creating and implementing manpower plans.

The line manager
It is important that the line manager has a key involvement in the process. This book has made few references to a 'manpower planner', and specialists must not take over. The line manager knows best what resources he needs to do the work expected of him and should be given considerable freedom in getting them.

Why is it not appropriate to give the line manager the resouces he needs instead of increasing his overheads with services? The answer lies in the increasing complexity which faces the organization. The emergence of strong interest groups in all fields, from government to trade unions, together with the heightening expectations people have of society make greater cohesion necessary for organizations across a whole range of activities. It is an effect (and cause) of complexity that any job requires the finer balancing of conflicting forces than was necessary before. Uncertainty about supply, about markets and resources, from raw materials to employees, leads the organization to design strategies for keeping them in balance. But the line manager will not be able to play a complete role at the strategic/policy making stage. Strategy is concernd with the overall direction of the whole organization and the line manager is only one part of the organization. He may have to let some of his options be subjugated to the options of other line managers in the interests of the organization as a whole. This can happen in a number of areas. If one department has surplus manpower it might be possible to retrain and then redeploy them in another department. To be achieved effectively, such a policy will need central direction and co-ordination.

The problems caused may restrict the receiving line manager but may be outweighted by the benefits to the organization as a whole.

There are thus areas where the line manager has responsibility for manpower planning but it is essential that this planning should take place within an overall co-ordinated framework. This need for an overall framework to ensure that manpower policies are integrated requires the attention of an overall controlling and co-ordinating function.

Corporate planning and finance

Where is the overall co-ordinating function to come from? There are a number of possibilities and advantages and disadvantages associated with each. For may organizations such discussion may be academic. In practice the organizational location may be the result of

117

historical accident, perhaps reflecting the early efforts in the field.

One alternative is within the corporate planning function. Many organizations will not have a department with this name and even fewer that have will be acquainted with the activity. Corporate planning is what is happening when management across the organization is working towards common objectives properly linking together the managing of all resources. Where a department has attempted to encourage this type of activity it is natural that it should have attempted to include manpower planning.

The main problems of locating manpower planning in this department is that their interest is more naturally directed towards economic and financial resource management. It is suggested that to treat people simply as a financial or economic resource (even worse a liability) is unnecessarily restricting and anyway will run into trade union problems.

It is possible to argue in favour of locating manpower planning activity within the finance function. Unlike corporate planning, all organizations have such a department. Also, organizations are judged against financial criteria and manpower costs are becoming an important determinant of the financial success of many organizations.

Manpower decisions are not affected directly by cost but by recruiting or not recruiting, which in turn affects costs. If these manpower decisions are to be managed the organization needs a function which is closely associated with people decisions across the organization as a whole.

Personnel department

There are strong arguments for the personnel function having the overall controlling responsibility for manpower planning. It is the only department which looks at manpower across the organization as a whole. It is the only function closely and exclusively associated with the manpower resource. The finance department may do something similar but their concern is with finance, not man-management. Manpower planning is concerned with integrated planning decisions in respect of recruitment, training, industrial relations and so on and the personnel function is nearest to those decisions, best understands them and, hopefully, should be in a position to encourage their integration.

Having said that, reservations remain. The personnel function does not have a history of involvement in planning. It has been criticized for its over-concern with short term problems and for a failure to take account of the future effect of present decisions, though all functions can be criticized in this respect. Many of the skills in manpower planning require a degree of numeracy not always a skill associated with personnel managers. Finally, many personnel managers are not part of the top management team and the manpower interest is often not represented at board level (except of course when a crisis, such as a labour dispute, has to be dealt with). Without this representation at the highest level the ultimate effect of manpower planning on the organization will be limited.

This has changed and the personnel manager has earned a place at board level by performance and the realization that employees are *the* key resource. He will also have to earn respect for the manpower questions he raises when he is there — not a simple task in the face of entrenched attitudes from other functions who may well regard manpower as an unfortunately necessary liability.

It is being argued that a need exists for a central executive authority to bring the various aspects of manpower in the organization together. This need is amplified by the Sony car illustration shown in Figure 30. If a group of people designed parts for a car without reference to one another the sony car might well result. Of course the car is out of balance and will not work effectively. Indeed the strains imposed by the inconsistences may lead to a total breakdown. In personnel terms these inconsistences which lead to strains might well be the problems of differentials between occupation groups or departments. The personnel manager is well aware that the friction can lead to a breakdown, namely a strike or more hidden form of conflict.

A central body is therefore needed and since the problems are personnel problems the personnel department is an obvious choice. Current thinking seems to support this view though three or four years ago the personnel function was very reluctant to enter the world of strategies and executive authority. It is worth restating that the consequences of an over zealous approach to central executive authority from a non-line department may be expensive and even fatal for the organization. The problem for personnel managers is not to inhibit unnecessarily the people who are producing wealth — both managers and the employees

FIGURE 30

on the shop floor. The over self-indulgence of proud professionals, be they accountants, lawyers, economists or personnel managers, must rank highly as having a damaging effect on our prosperity. This indulgence really must stop.

Having considered who is to co-ordinate the manpower planning activity it is appropriate to look at what the effort is concerned with.

The flexible manpower plan

There should be a degree of reluctance to use a phrase such as the 'manpower plan'. It implies inflexibility, something that is fixed and unchanging; a document that lies in a cupboard to be done again a year later when the revised 'plan' is also put in the cupboard. Manpower planning is a process rather than a plan or a simple definable document. The process is continuous adaptation to change. Therefore, the 'plan' is no more than a photograph of the position at a certain time which may help to concentrate managerial minds on the decisions that have to be made over a few months but it should not constrain those minds from a continuous review of the effects of change.

How should the manager begin in formulating a plan? It may be useful to have some overall statement of the organization's manpower objectives. It will be impossible to raise a perfectly satisfactory statement but the attempt should lead to more intelligent discussion of manpower problems. The manpower objective should be seen in conjunction with the organization's overall objective which may be to make a certain profit or provide a level of service to the customer.

Importance of assumptions

The second part of the plan should cover assumptions and policy directions. It is helpful to set out the background against which the planning is taking place.

121

These assumptions may cover a variety of areas, such as what is expected to happen to unemployment and its consequent effect on wastage or labour market trends. Policy directions should be an explicit statement of what strategic and policy decisions have been made. These must be made readily available if managers are to plan within them. The assumptions have a number of purposes:

to provide a common framework for all managers
to set out the organization's policy intentions
to set out areas of developing policy and to encourage managers to consider new areas when planning.

FIGURE 31

Examples of assumptions for manpower planning

Expected unemployment rates over the period of the forecast

Effect of market and production plans on manpower

Areas of overmanning and targets for productivity increases

Policy and constraints on contractors and agency staff — use of overtime

Promotion policies and desirability of cross functional movement

Remuneration policies

Balance between external recruitment and internal promotion

Future conditions in respect of holidays

Allowances for sickness, absenteeism and disputes

Expected output from the education system and its effect

Supply of labour in the local labour market

External economic factors and effect on manpower

Employment of women and extension of female opportunities

Apprentice and student pass rates at colleges

In Figure 31 are listed a range of assumptions which managers should have in mind when undertaking planning. It is worth remembering that even in areas where it is difficult to make an assessment the effort will probably be worthwhile. Not only will management understanding be increased but a measure will be available against which to compare future events.

Preparing the forecast
It has been noted in the chapters concerning supply and demand that the organization should concentrate its forecasts on those areas crucial to its success. The temptation to classify manpower into a whole range of categories must be avoided. The exercise will become too complicated and management will lose its enthusiasm for it.

It is therefore necessary to look at the organization's manpower and select carefully the areas which seem important to the firms operation. Consideration should be given to the lead-time for training and development. It will be important to forecast in respect of chemical engineers if they are important in the organization for they take a long time to train and develop, whereas the general availability of labourers may make that a less important category to forecast in advance.

The effect of the external environment should not be neglected. If there is a scarcity of a particular skill in the labour market it may be essential that the organization identifies its future requirements and considers how it will meet them.

The result of this exercise might lead to forecasts being raised for workload, numbers employed, recruitment and wastage and perhaps training. An example of a forecast is given in Figure 32. While this is not ideal and is probably lacking in appropriate detail (the occupation categories are too broad) it will serve as

123

FIGURE 32
Manpower forecasts

Department and occupation	actual	contract	budget year 1	year 2	year 3	year 4
EMPLOYEES — ACTUAL			**FORECAST (2-4 YEARS)**			
SALES						
managers						
technical						
clerical						
craft						
other manual						
TOTAL						
MAINTENANCE						
managers						
technical						
clerical						
craft						
other manual						
TOTAL						
SERVICES						
managers						
technical						
clerical						
craft						
other manual						
TOTAL						
GRAND TOTAL						
KEY RECRUITMENT						
graduates						
school/college						
apprentices						
adult recruits						
KEY TRAINING						
adult recruits						
apprentices						
WASTAGE						
managers						
fitters						
manuals						

a guide for those organizations new to forecasting manpower requirements and the supply of them.

Having determined the forecast the plans available to meet them must be considered.

Plans for recruitment

When taking into account current manpower employed and expected wastage levels, the forecast of manpower levels will give an indication of recruitment needs. There are a number of important choices:

recruitment from outside the organization
recruitment from other divisions within the organization
promotion from within the division
promotion from within the department

The problems of each have been looked at under the chapter on supply forecasting. It can be seen that the planning decisions are not separate from others. An investigation of recruitment requirements quickly raises problems of the suitability of existing employees and results in a need to explore promotion possibilities.

Plans for promotion

In many ways this is the obverse of the need to recruit and a balance must be struck. The manager will be concerned with a number of factors:

are current employees suitable for promoting?
can they become suitable with training and development?
what have past promotion patterns been?
how will past patterns affect future intentions?

At the end of this exercise the manager should be aware of his promotion priorities and better prepared to form plans in the other personnel policy areas.

Plans for training

Training cannot really be undertaken without a knowledge of future requirements and where they are to come from. Is the organization to recruit 'ready-made' employees from the labour market or will it recruit employees who will need to be trained first? Perhaps employees from other parts of the organization are to be promoted who will need to be retrained. The trainer needs to know what he needs for both buildings and trainers. All this means a knowledge of future manpower requirements and the plans for achieving them. The training manager should be fully involved in determining manpower plans. Apart from knowing what resources he needs, he should be able to advise on efficient ways of deploying manpower and of meeting requirements.

A great deal of the training undertaken will emerge directly from the forecasts themselves and more will be implicit. It is a mistake to see training as separate from this planning process and the training managers should be closely involved within it and should provide help and advice.

An article in *Personnel Management*[40] showed how training could be undertaken counter cyclicly to economic activity; that is, when activity was high and sales booming, training could be limited so that the maximum number of employees were available to do the necessary work. When activity was low, training could be increased thus taking up spare employee capacity, perhaps avoiding lay-offs and adding to the skills of the organization's manpower so that maximum advantage could be taken when expansion began again.

Plans for management and organization development

Plans will also be required for management (indeed employees') personal development.

126

Management development is both an input and an output in the process of formulating manpower plans. The organization needs to be aware of the constraints imposed on it by the present managerial force in terms of the range of skills and abilities they possess. This is an input and should be highlighted at the investigation stage.

The formulation of manpower plans affects management development because the organization's objectives in terms of markets, production or service to the customer will be achieved largely through the efforts of its managers. Most organizations can expect to experience rapid and dramatic change, and management development can be seen as a way of maintaining and impoving managerial performance in the face of the problems it brings.

The plans for management and organization development will cover:

preparing managers for change
avoiding creating unrealistic expectations
creating expectations where appropriate
highlighting areas where improved performance is needed
succession planning and priorities, both individual and group
need for change in organization culture
dealing with motivational problems
encouraging identification and meeting of objectives for each manager emerging from business plans.

Plans for costs and productivity
Factors affecting labour productivity are discussed in chapter 8. Plans for costs and productivity will cover a number of areas. The organization's market and pro-

duction plans may well rely on meeting certain cost constraints. These cost items must be highlighted and management must be controlled against them. Cost factors may cover a variety of items such as:

the reduction of cost of administrative support

the reduction of wastage costs

the reduction of labour costs per unit of output/sales.

Unfortunately few manpower plans have cost expressions and one suspects this is a major area for development in the future.

Productivity plans may well be associated with cost constraints in that they may be expected to achieve a cost reduction. It also needs to be stressed that plans and priorities for productivity schemes should emerge from the organization's business plans.

Plans for remuneration
There is no point in highlighting cohesive plans for recruitment, promotion and development if the organization does not pay its employees properly. This is not simply paying sufficiently well to avoid losing employees but means maintaining a balance within the firm itself. A remuneration expert is necessary to set out the constraints and be aware of the background against which he is working.

Plans for retirements and redundancy and planned run-down
If the organization finds that it has excess manpower and cannot avoid a reduction in manpower levels, at least the planning process should avoid the harmful social consequences of sudden redundancies. Planning provides every prospect that employees can be retrained to other jobs within the organization. Recruitment can be limited so that unnecessary redundancies are avoided. By using natural wastage, redun-

dancy may well be avoided if anticipated sufficiently well in advance. Retirements may be encouraged for older employees and a generous redundancy scheme worked out. It may also be possible to make use of opportunities in other firms or even other areas and the government's employment agencies offer help.

Plans for industrial relations

In view of the importance and the precarious state of industrial relations in a developing political climate it is the one field of personnel management that may well justify a planning unit of its own. It should of course be involved in the planning process as a whole or both activities are liable to operate in an unrealistic world. The involvement of industrial relations will depend considerably on the political situation in which the firm finds itself in relation to employees and trade unions. The more complex and potentially explosive, the more necessary it becomes to have an industrial relations strategy.

Industrial relations plans will cover all the aspects referred to earlier, such as recruitment, pay strategies (what can be afforded; what will the unions accept) and redundancy (will disputes and sit-ins be the result). Due to the sensitivity of these factors, close and high-level attention will have to be given to industrial relations strategy making.

Having formulated plans in all these areas, accommodation and other physical resources must be considered. The requirement for offices should relate to the numbers of people to be employed; equally it is no use having employees if the equipment they need is not available.

Narrative statement and manpower report

Next, the whole must be drawn together in a form that can be used to stimulate discussion throughout the

129

organization. A manager should be aware of his own responsibilities in detail though he would also probably find it helpful to have some knowledge of the organization's intentions.

Because all manpower aspects cannot be expressed adequately in numerical form it is useful to prepare a narrative statement of the organization's intentions. This may well act as an introduction to a document discussed with managers.

Involvement of employees and trade unions in formulating plans

Limited reference only has been made to the involvement of trade unions and employees in formulating plans.

A number of organizations do involve their trade union in planning to some extent but a larger number would prefer not to! Basic mistrust by management and trade unions of each other's motives make real progress by mutual agreement unlikely. Most organizations will enter the arena only if forced to and then quite unprepared, first in providing information and then in setting objectives and priorities. Both sides may still be carrying out a ritual more appropriate to earlier days of power and influence than to our present modest circumstances. There should be no dispute about the desirability of involving employees in decisions that affect them. Many managers appear to be living through a private virility ritual, with the trade unions cast in the role of the beast.

If the trade unions have not the necessary wisdom to be involved in 'planning' many companies will look directly to their employees. (It should also be remembered that many companies and organizations do not have 'shop floor' trade unionism anyway.) This focus on employees is the driving force behind 'excellence' in companies (see Supplementary Reading List).

Human resource management — as this focus has come to be known — sees employee relations and industrial relations as different spheres of personnel activity. The argument goes that commitment and flexibility from people are the best way to ensure continuity and success.

In preparing 'plans', the need for flexibility has been stressed. The document prepared once a year may have value but will quickly become out of date. The manager should instead be working towards a continuous review of the organization's changing manpower requirements against economic and social values and criteria that are themselves changing. Plans should therefore be brief, though the studies and analyses backing them up may be more detailed. In this way a dialogue within the organization continually updates the manpower picture, raising new issues and dealing with problems.

7 Manpower control, reporting and costing

Management implies control. If the manager is not monitoring the various elements of manpower within his firm he will not know if he is achieving his objectives. In practice all organizations have some method of manpower control. The purpose of this chapter is to question whether the approaches in general use are appropriate to current needs, in a situation where manpower is more critical to the successful running of organizations than it has ever been before.

Approaches to manpower control
What is meant by 'control'? To most people the word implies restriction, often known as 'establishment control'. To others it will imply a passive monitoring. It is possible to base systems of manpower control on either of these two approaches. The first will probably achieve adherence to a set standard but may limit initiative and flexibility, both extremely necessary in the present changing and uncertain environment. The second may be unwisely passive and, without any built-in response mechanism, will be slow to respond to need. Examples of both these approaches working in practice will be given later in this chapter.

What is required is an approach to manpower control which is rigorous and meets objectives without being

FIGURE 33(a)
Control

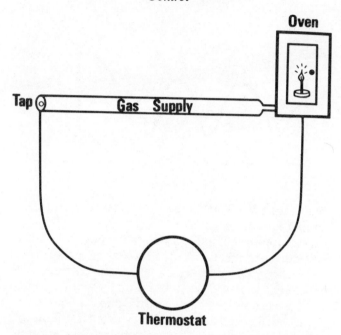

unnecessarily and destructively restrictive.

The nature of control may best be explained by reference to the control exercised by a thermostat in an oven. In the diagram in Figure 33(a) the object is to bake the cake in the oven. To do this a certain temperature must be maintained. Consequently the thermostat is set and it regulates the supply of gas to the oven by turning the tap off and on. In manpower terms the control procedure should monitor personnel activity, such as the numbers employed and their productivity to meet a given objective, say the production of so many motor vehicles or the provision of a given service. The control procedure should be close enough to the power in the

133

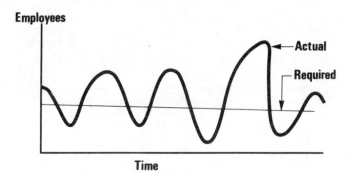

FIGURE 33(b)
Hunting

organization to effect short and long term recruitment, training and other personnel activities.

It is important to avoid a situation where the control procedure overreacts. In such a situation a shortage is met by a sudden surge, which results in a cutback. The consequent shortage results in a further surge and so on. In the example of baking a cake this would result in a burnt outside and a sad middle. The organization will have similar problems. This problem is called 'hunting' by engineers and is illustrated in Figure 33(b). It is a phenomenon known to all recruiters who struggle one year to recruit every apprentice or graduate they can only to be told the next year to turn away many good applicants.

The diagrammatic representations given here simplify the problem of control in personnel management. It is neither desirable nor possible to turn manpower off and on like a tap. Nevertheless these examples should serve to illustrate the general principle involved.

Why undertake manpower control?
The reasons for putting effort into developing systems

for manpower control relate closely to those for undertaking manpower planning itself. Having determined the organization's overall objectives and a strategy for achieving them, it is essential that there is some method of ensuring that what is wanted happens. In a rapidly changing environment, new situations are likely to arise. If the unforeseen is to be adequately met, the organization must have a sufficiently flexible control procedure to meet new situations.

What is to be controlled?

As well as the general approach the manager has to decide the 'units' in which he will control. This is not so simple as it sounds and there are a number of alternatives which are not necessarily mutually exclusive. These are:

1. control against head-counts-establishment
2. control against man-time (eg man hours, days etc)
3. control against costs
4. control against manning ratios of productivity
5. control against elements of each of the above

In addition, the manager has to decide how much he will control each of these in absolute terms (eg numbers employed in a plant) or in change terms (eg + or −) or percentage increase, decrease over a certain period. Unless all manpower is to be justified completely at each review period, a system of monitoring the degree of change may be useful as an intermediary measure.

1 Head-counts – establishment

This is the method of control with which managers will be most familiar (see Figure 34). It is a simple idea to understand and expresses manpower in common language. It has the advantage that seeing recruitment and leaving in this way — making 10 employees redundant

135

FIGURE 34
Establishment control

Section	Number Employed	Establishment	Difference
Marketing Department			
Manuals			
Gas fitters	87	94	−7
Apprentices	11	12	−1
Maintenance men	22	27	−5
Handymen	9	6	+3
	129	139	−10
Staff (technical/admin)			
Managers	1	1	—
Asst managers	1	1	—
Technical engineer I	3	2	+1
Technical engineer II	4	7	−3
Foremen	9	11	−2
	18	22	−4
Staff (clerical)			
Section heads	1	1	—
Deputies	1	1	—
Clerks I	3	4	−1
Clerks II	7	9	−2
	12	15	−3

rather than cutting costs by £x,000's — will probably bring a manager nearer to real issues.

In practice the effect is a more direct control of manpower. This method also avoids the problem of cost allocation where it becomes possible to achieve 'paper' cost reductions in manpower without reducing numbers.

Inflexibility is the major weakness of establishment control. Work is not static and yet the establishment is unlikely to anticipate the changes in the work to be done. The manager may therefore protect himself by constantly exaggerating his requirements, thus allowing himself a safety margin of 'fat' in case it should be needed. The problem is that the 'fat' reduces the likelihood of pressure being applied to work efficiency and poor utilization is the long-term result.

If the establishment is seen as an upper limit, it will not represent a forecast of what is expected to happen and so will be of limited value for determining recruitment, training and other manpower strategies. Another aspect which arises from the inflexibility of establishments occurs from the establishment being seen as the top limit. The result is that a manager must justify additions to his establishment, but not any recruitment required to meet it.

Head-counting tends to lack discrimination between separate categories of manpower so that manpower dissimilar both in occupation and costs is grouped together: this can present a further limitation. It is not easy or even desirable to control manpower against all separate occupations in the organization. Even if the system of classifying occupations makes this possible, the system will become too complex for the manager to assimilate and respond to quickly. It is therefore necessary to decide which occupations should be highlighted. These will change from time to time and will need to be kept under constant review.

The head-count system counts only employees but manpower employed can be supplemented by the use of overtime, contract and agency employees. Supplementary analyses will also be required. Otherwise managers restricted by the control procedure from recruiting may circumvent it by taking on agency staff. Even in organizations where cost information supplements head-counting it is not uncommon to find costs of agencies and contractors classified in a way that separates them from manpower and wages paid.

Finally, it should be remembered that a key purpose of undertaking manpower planning is to achieve better use of manpower. It is therefore necessary to supplement head-counts with information on the effectiveness of the workforce. This information will include losses due to sickness, accidents, absenteeism and other causes which significantly affect manning levels. Effectiveness in terms of achievement of results should also be highlighted. It is no good reducing manpower costs if the result is an unacceptable decline in the achievement of results and the service offered to the customer.

To summarize, the disadvantages of manpower control by establishments (and indeed of central procedures in general use) are that:

1 it implies and encourages *maximum* rather than acceptable levels of manpower
2 it may be unrelated to *actual* employment over time if movements are not also controlled
3 it does not lead to regular review of *total* needs, only of upward changes. Tradition becomes the substitute for rigorous and frequent reviews of needs
4 forecasts, objectives and work change over time and if the establishment is fixed these changes are not reflected. The establishment does not anticipate the situation beyond the present
5 When manpower is to be reduced there may be no control at all. During expansion the system may work. But most organizations either need to *reduce* numbers or *change* to another type of manpower. The establishment being fixed in the present and monitoring only additions has no effect
6 establishments take no account of cost, productivity or performance
7 the managerial reward structure is based on the need to keep *below* establishment or rather not go

above it. A manager is penalized for going above and consequently he exaggerates the need to protect himself; this is also a means of defending himself against inflexibility in the system where additions take too long to be agreed

8 establishment systems are rarely successful in controlling manual occupations. They are usually in large stable monolithic organizations where manpower requirements are stable — even though they should not be. It is frequent to read of firms who have faced a crisis that results in major changes, often in manpower levels. A system of manpower control that exerts sufficient self-discipline on managers is required so that surgery is not necessary

9 the penalties for going over establishment are absolute and do not relate to the *reasons* for going over establishment.

2 Employee-time

Such methods of control involve expressing employees as effective units of time. This means that employees are expressed in terms of effective employee hours, days or years, as shown in Figure 35. It has the advantage of relating employees to the work they do, so concentrating on utilization. It can be particularly helpful for forecasting purposes where the forecast prepared is in terms of employee-time rather than employees. It may be more suitable where the work being undertaken is measurable in these terms and where the measurement is appropriate, as in a straighforward self-contained job such as installing an engine or undertaking a scheduled maintenance, though perhaps less so in managerial positions where output is less sensibly measured in terms of employee-time. Against this must be noted the difficulty of converting employees and jobs into units. The degree of accuracy is often more illusory than real. Another aspect of the same point is the risk of diverting managerial attention away from the management of people themselves — where the real problems are likely to lie. Except in the use of contractors and overtime, employee levels are not achieved through analysis and buying of hours as such but through the employment of people. That is where management's attention needs to be directed.

FIGURE 35
Control by man-time

Step A Convert employees available, overtime use of contractors into man hours; remember to allow fewer for part-timers

Step B Undertake budgets and forecasts in terms of man hours allowing for the use of overtime, contractors, part-timers, and absence from the work due to sickness and training.

Step C Present to management in tabular form as follows:

4 week monthly
analysis

Employee Classification	This month hours available	This month hours losses	%	Actual hours available	Target hours	% difference from target
Managerial	154	—	—	154	154	—
Technical support	870	110	12.6	760	640	+18.8
Clerical	210	—	—	210	280	−25.0
Craft	6,480	840	13.0	5,640	5,750	−2.0
Manual support	950	48	5.1	902	750	+20.3
TOTAL	8,664	998	11.5	7,666	7,574	+1.2
Training		768	—			
Sickness		230	—			
Other		—	—			

Step D Discuss problems with managers and take remedial action. In this example the reason for increases in technical and manual support services could be investigated.

(The reader who wishes to study this subject further can contact the IMS at the University of Sussex. From where much of the background to this section has been drawn).

3 Costs

An example of controlling manpower against costs is given in Figure 36

FIGURE 36
Control by costs

Step A Convert employees into costs splitting between direct (wages, bonuses etc.) and indirect (recruitment, training).

Step B Undertake budgets and forecasts in terms of direct and indirect costs

Step C Present to management in tabular form as follows:

Subject	Actual Wages and bonuses £	This month Other £	Total year to date £	This month Total £	Target year to date Total £	% Difference from year
Managers	370	—	1,184	370	1,070	+10.6
Technical support	1,760	320	5,692	1,840	6,240	−8.8
Clerical	190	74	806	210	780	+3.3
Craft	5,280	140	16,740	4,620	15,940	+5.0
Manual support	1,020	87	3,950	850	3,650	+8.2
	8,620	621	28,372	7,890	27,680	+2.5

Step D Establish procedure to discuss problems with managers

Many of the advantages and disadvantages of controlling manpower against costs have been given above. It has the advantage of direct relationship to financial criteria against which the success of the organization will substantially be judged. But costing of manpower is so poorly developed it may be difficult to achieve in practice. Making decisions based on such aspects as wages will be a temptation, which may not be the most economic action in the longer term (see Figure 37). The Figure analyses the alternative costs of either providing a driver's mate to help unload goods from a vehicle or of a mechanical attachment to achieve the same end. The correct decision in 1971 might have seemed to be to have an employee to do the work rather than invest in a

141

more expensive vehicle but, by 1977, manpower costs have increased dramatically whereas in real terms capital costs of the vehicle have fallen; consequently in 1977 the economic decision is to substitute capital for labour.

FIGURE 37
Capital or labour?

	1971	1973	1977
Annual cost of labour saving capital investment	1200	1180	1160
Cost of person	1150	1190	1590

£s at constant 1971 prices

The difficulties in changing policy, such as trade union reaction to redundancy and the cost of severance payments, may mean that the correct decision in 1971 was to use machinery and not employ drivers' mates. The implication is that an analysis of change over time may affect what seems to be the right decision today. Such an approach is difficult to adopt without giving attention to planning manpower and controlling those plans against costs.

4 Employment ratios of productivity

Control against productivity indices is attractive. It concentrates attention on an important area, utilization. If the poor productivity performance which will exist in many organizations is to be dealt with, some measure of utilization will be required. Head-counts or costs attempt to control against some arbitrary factor without considering how effective extra employment or extra expenditure is. It is probably common practice but a manager should not be criticized for employing more people or incurring greater costs without reference to what has been produced as a result. Another use of ratios is that comparisons across departments or divisions become possible which can highlight opportunities for improvement. In addition they become particularly useful when ratios are being used to prepare forecasts of manpower. Examples of using many ratios are given in Figure 38. But productivity indicators may be difficult to derive and divert attention from recruitment, promotion and other personnel decisions.

FIGURE 38
Control by productivity indicator

Step A Ascertain relevant indicators of employees' productivity. This may relate to cost, hours, output sales revenue etc, and so on.

Step B Undertake budgets and forecasts in terms of the indicators

Step C Present to management in tabular form. It is useful to be able to compare one department with another doing the same kind of work if this is possible.

	District A		District B	
	Actual this month	Target this month	Actual this month	Target this month
Jobs per district employee	94.7	88.0	91.4	89.0
Technical support per 100 district employees	1.2	1.1	1.4	1.1
Clerical per 100 district employees	2.7	2.9	3.0	2.9

Step D Discuss problems with management. It may also be useful to show previous years to give trends. The reasons for apparent differences in productivity can be investigated

Integrated manpower control

The control procedure suggested in Figure 39 should be regarded as a framework within which the manager can develop his own. The manager will have practical difficulties in trying to develop any system, particularly if it crosses established principles in the organization. For instance, the costs aspect will probably be covered in part by established financial procedures though

FIGURE 39
Framework for manpower control

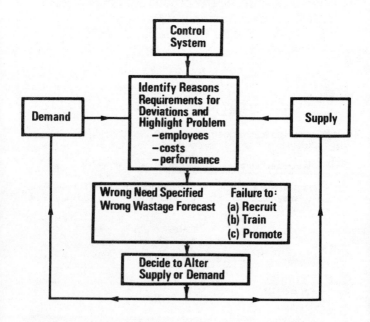

whether it will be adequate for manpower control may be less certain. The accountant may be reluctant to agree to a change that is not directly in his function's interest. Another problem may relate to the organization's previous practice. Where rigid establishment control has been operated, with consequent penalties for going over establishment, it is not likely that a flexible open system which relies more on managerial judgement will meet with immediate success.

All the methods of controlling manpower given above have value. Often they are limited by not being able to cover all the aspects which the manager needs to control.

In addition the procedure should have the following features:

1 flexibility to meet new situations
2 it should relate to the organization's planning objectives and procedure
3 it should relate to financial and productivity criteria
4 it should result in action to solve identified problems

The following paragraphs amplify what is meant by each of these features.

1 Need for flexibility

The need for flexibility to meet new situations is important in a rapidly changing environment where forecasting of future manning levels is a precarious occupation. The manager must be free to alter his manning levels if the situation demands it — for example work to be done increases or decreases but this does not imply licence. Any change must be justified and a rigorous analysis of why it was not seen earlier should be undertaken. The need for flexibility also suggests that the procedure to effect a change should be capable of swift operation.

2 Relation to planning objectives and procedure

The control procedure should be seen as part of the planning process within the organization. The purpose is for short to medium term manpower management designed to ensure that longer term objectives are being met and sensible adjustments being made in the short term in the face of practical difficulties. It is therefore necessary for the systems to be interrelated with the experience in one affecting what happens in the other.

3 Relation to financial and productivity criteria

With increasingly complex organizations, complex control procedures become necessary. It is not possible to control manpower levels within themselves without reference to complicating factors such as cost and productivity criteria. It is not sufficient to agree a manning level with a manager and control against it. The manager may keep within his manpower budget but if he fails to contain costs or meet output targets he may well have failed. They cannot be considered separately for the cause of failure in one may result from achieving the other.

4 Action to solve identified problems

Many control procedures are too passive. There is limited value in comparing actual with intended if the cause of any difference is not identified and dealt with. Consequently the control procedure must relate to the organization's overall objectives so that any failure to achieve them is brought out. It must also be possible to find out how a problem identified through the control procedure came about: was it a failure to recruit or train or was wastage forecast incorrectly? Finally it should be possible to discuss with appropriate managers ways of meeting the present situation (say through additional training or recruitment or dismissals) and of ways of reducing the likelihood of a recurrence.

Having considered the factors which require control and noted the desired features of the control procedures, a suitable framework will have to be established. All procedures must be adapted to meet the needs of individual organizations but the framework given in Figure 39 may help. Here, the basic purpose of the control procedure is to ensure that there is sufficient (and not too much) manpower available to meet the organization's objectives expressed through the demand for manpower. The procedure shown is not passive but identifies the extent of and reasons for deviations from requirement and indeed for the requirement itself. It highlights difficulties of employment, cost and performance and converts these into manpower policy problems. In this way the problem is expressed as a failure to recruit and train the numbers and quality required (or perhaps recruiting and training too many). Alternatively, surplus or shortage of manpower may result from a wrong forecast of wastage. The final stage is to take remedial action. This covers three areas:

remedy present problems
anticipate emerging problems
avoid problem occurring again.

These may affect either supply or demand; for example more recruitment or training might be undertaken or the specified need for manpower might be changed. In each case responsibility is allocated to the appropriate manager and each is aware of what is needed. Decisions are thus made to change the need specified, the way of

147

meeting it or both. The control procedure can operate tactically to meet a new need or an old one not fulfilled, or strategically to question the manpower need specified in terms of either requirements or recruitment, training, promotion and development to meet a requirement. In practice it is sensible to arrange formal systems by which progress towards meeting objectives is reported to managers. A sample document is given in Figure 40 (b). The procedure is shown in Figure 40 (a) and is drawn from that set out by R L Worsfold formerly of British Gas.

It is probably necessary to have a simple summary such as this backed up by more detailed analyses of various sections. It is useful to prepare reports for each cost centre, district or department so that the reports can be discussed with the managers concerned.

The purpose of manpower control is to help the organization meet its manpower requirements and in turn its overall objectives. It is not a passive monitoring

FIGURE 40(a)
Procedure for manpower control

Control against:
    head counts
    costs
    ratios of productivity
Procedure to be followed—the four principles:
    responsibility of function director to determine need
    discuss need with personnel who co-ordinate
    executive (board) agree overall budget and forecasts
    personnel monitor targets and initiate executive
        action.

This may be supplemented by the document given in figure 40(b)

FIGURE 40(b)

Step A Determine relevant factors, eg employees, use of contractors and overtime, wastage and recruitment

Step B Consider how to account for other factors such as workload and costs (this can be done in narrative form)

Step C Undertake budget and forecasts using criteria established in Step A

Step D Present to management in tabular form

Occupation or department	Employees	Deviation from expected	Overtime and contractors used	Wastage	Recruitment	Trainees completing courses	Training shortfall
Dept A	50	+4	—	3	7	4	—
Dept B	39	−7	3	12	8	2	6

Step E Discuss problems with management. For instance are the extra four employees in department A justified by increased work. Why was the high wastage in B not foreseen? Look at forecasting methods. Is department B not meeting its work targets? Why were insufficient recruits taken on? Why did insufficient numbers pass through training? Review recruitment and training methods.

but a dynamic system that highlights problems, allocates responsibility and prepares resulting action to alleviate current problems and avoid recurrences. It is a system in which all parts of the organization share and in which each is aware of his own contribution and the effect on the whole of his individual failure to achieve expected results.

Manpower costs

Normal accounting practice treats expenditure in two ways:

149

the item is brought into the profit and loss account
and written off in the current accounting period
the item is regarded as an asset and is brought into
the profit and loss account over a number of years.

The first is often called current account and the second
capital account. In the first stationery or equipment
bought and used in one period are included. In the
second account purchases such as machinery which
may be paid for in one period but are used over many
succeeding periods are written off over a number of
periods. Manpower expenditure is normally always
included in the first account. It is therefore not counted
as a continuing asset but as cost to be written off against
profit immediately.

The method has the advantage that large capital
expense paid for in one period would otherwise distort
that profit/loss account and would give an untrue picture of the organization's performance.

This treatment of manpower as a cost rather than as
an asset probably has its roots in the regard in which
labour was held when accounting conventions were
established. The prime concern of management at the
time was the use of machinery and the proper exploitation of expensive investment. In comparison manpower
was poorly regarded, the object being to replace it with
an efficient machine wherever possible. Manpower was
a cost and capital was an asset and generated the
income.

A tendency to ignore hidden costs presents another
problem. The actual expenditure on advertising or personnel costs may be small in relation to the costs of line
manager's time in interviewing and sifting applications.
Effort has recently been made to develop knowledge in
this area, notably by the Manpower Society working
party on manpower costs. It has raised a checklist of
150

costs given in Figure 41 (the full papers from this study were never published). Even this list is not exhaustive; it does not include accommodation costs which, for many firms (especially in London and other cities), are a major consideration. Most organizations will not have such a range of information available, especially relating to different occupations in the organization. Nevertheless it should be possible to exploit available systems to make some useful progress.

FIGURE 41
Manpower costs checklist

Origin of Costs: A checklist of headings under which costs arise

1. **REMUNERATION**
1.1 Salary costs
1.1a Basic pay
1.1b Bonus payments
1.1c Overtime
1.1d Supplementary payments, eg shift pay, dirt pay, etc
1.1e Merit awards
1.1f Temporary replacements for holidays, sickness etc
1.2 Direct fringe benefits
1.2a Car
1.2b Pension fund contribution
1.2c Luncheon vouchers/subsidised meals
1.2d Educational support for children of employees
1.2e Subscriptions to professional bodies
1.2f Subsidised housing including loans at preferential rates, special mortgage
1.2g Subsidised travel via loans to buy cars etc
1.2h Season ticket loans
1.2i Share ownership schemes
1.2j Location/assignment weighting
1.2k Holiday—statutory
—personal days
—sabbatical
—other discretionary paid vacation
1.3 Statutory costs
1.3a National Insurance contributions
1.3b Graduated pension contributions
1.3c Selective Employment Tax (regional and industrial payments must be offset against this)
1.3d Training board contributions (offset by grants, see section 3)
1.3e Employers' liability
1.3f Other statutory levies
2. **RECRUITMENT COSTS** — applicable to avoidable and unavoidable turnover as well as to new jobs
2.1 Pre-recruitment
2.1a Preparation or review of specifications for both the job to be done and the person to be recruited

151

2.1b Briefing of personnel officer (and advertising staff) with line manager
2.1c Preparation of recruitment programme
2.2 Search
2.2a All indirect promotional/advertising effort directed at furthering recruitment
2.2b All direct promotional/advertising effort directed at furthering recruitment including job advertising, stationery, postage, documentation of recruitment records and related administration costs
2.2c Head hunting costs
2.3 Candidate evaluation
2.3a Interviewing including travelling, hospitality and the university/college round
2.3b Bought in selection costs
—briefing
—advertising
—preliminary selection
—complete selection
2.3c Selection tests either bought or created and including costs of subsequent administration
2.4 Induction
2.4a Inducement to move
2.4b Medical examination prior to establishment procedure
2.4c Orientation

3. TRAINING COSTS — offset by grants
3.1 Induction period
3.2 Remuneration of trainee and trainer
3.3 Expenses of trainee and trainer including travel and subsistence
3.4 Books and materials used
3.5 Machines and buildings used in continuous training
3.6 Bought out training — school, college, government training centre fees
3.7 Development and maintenance of training programmes including cost

of staff in training departments when not actually engaged in direct training
3.8 Reports, appraisal costs of those people other than the trainee and trainer, eg counselling reviews
3.9 Training for retirements
3.10 Assimilation costs — the costs incurred of employing a person after induction but before he/she is fully proficient
3.11 Higher material wastage until trainee is fully experienced
3.12 Loss of possible production from trainer whilst he/she is engaged in training

4. RE-LOCATION COSTS — temporary and permanent
4.1 Hostel charges — long term
4.2 Hotel charges — short term
4.3 Direct disturbance allowance
4.4 Cost of disturbance, eg legal fees, removal costs
4.5 Premiums paid with regard to housing price differentials or house purchase assistance
4.6 Temporary travel subsidy
4.7 Travelling expenses
4.8 *Ex gratia* re-equipment costs incurred in moving house
*

5. LEAVING COSTS
5.1 Loss of production between loss and recruitment
5.2 Statutory redundancy payments (less rebates)
5.3 *Ex gratia* payments
5.4 Retirement payments (other than pensions)
5.5 Liquidation of direct fringe benefits could be plus or minus costs

6. SUPPORT COSTS
6.1 House magazine
6.2 Social club
6.3 Subsidy for other social activities

6.4 Medical welfare schemes
6.5 Canteens
6.6 Safety facilities
6.7 Long service awards
6.8 Suggestion schemes
6.9 Music-while-you-work
6.10 Security service
6.11 Schemes for preferential purchase of goods including costs in purchasing department
6.12 Insurance premiums
6.13 Library and information services
6.14 Use of firms resources for private ends (whether acknowledged or illicit)
6.15 General travel and entertaining expenses not specifically allocatable to a project
6.16 General background training not specifically allocatable to the job being done
6.17 Prestige accommodation
6.18 Car park costs
6.19 Death benefits
6.20 Rehabilitation/convalescent homes
6.21 Holiday homes

7. PERSONNEL ADMINISTRATION
7.1 Organized manpower records — these could be in more than one location in a company with decentralized company activities. These records include:
7.1a Personal record cards
7.1b Personal files
7.1c Salary administration records
7.1d Job specification
7.1e Manpower planning record
7.2 Salary review costs
7.3 Maintenance of industrial relations including consultative committees
7.4 Manpower research project costs

* NOTE: Leaving may give rise to recruitment and training costs, and sections 2, 3, and 5 should be considered together when considering cost of voluntary turnover.

(The checklist has been drawn up by the Manpower Society).

Attempts have recently been made to put this right and interesting techniques known as human asset and human resource accounting have been developed. No doubt more applications and subsequent refinements can be made. One suspects that while the basic premise — that of seeing manpower as an asset — is a good one there is some way to go before it can be adequately represented in a company's balance sheet, though examples of the method in use are available.[38].

Probably what is required (human resource management and better manpower costing help) is not so much a new set of accounting conventions as simply a change in attitude by management. If management looks on manpower as an income generator and not as a cost, it will set about motivating employees and releasing the effort, aspirations and creativity that lie in all people.

The people the organization employs are the primary source of income generation, are the only vehicles through which change and organizational objectives can be achieved, and are the only resource which can judge, integrate, create and take decisions. In short people are the only 'resource' which ensures the survival of the organization.

Manpower costs and assets are important areas for manpower planning. Gareth Stainer[2] noted that 'There are always plenty of sound practical reasons why nothing should be changed and accountants seem as good at finding them as anyone else.' A degree of caution is not a bad thing: if accountants rushed after every new gimmick one would fear for the financial stability of organizations. In manpower planning sensible manpower decisions must be backed up by a greater knowledge than usual of the costs. The manpower planner should encourage this movement and stimulate development. There may be accountants in the organization who would welcome the opportunity to study new areas. Finally, it is useful to compare how much specialist planning and research effort is spent on manpower appraisal in relation to capital appraisal. The organization may well wonder as a result whether sufficient resources are allocated to planning and controlling manpower resources.

8 Information for manpower planning

It is not possible to undertake good manpower planning without a sound information base. Lack of knowledge about manpower in the organization is the problem with which most aspiring manpower planners will have to deal. It is common for the initial period of involvement in manpower planning to be spent setting up adequate information flows. It has been argued that lack of information is the single most important barrier preventing organizations undertaking manpower planning. While there is some truth in this, each manager knows that if a requirement is specified it will probably be met. The lack of information about manpower springs from a general failure to tackle manpower problems. To suggest that lack of information is preventing eager managers from making progress in the manpower field is generous to the point of self-deceit. Until a need for information is specified none will be available.[7a]

Information is needed to make decisions. The type of information collected and its frequency is determined by the nature of the decisions. Because planning decisions need constant revision and review, a flow of information needs to be established that allows that review to take place.

Often the information is provided by someone else. This raises difficulties for the personnel department in particular but also for the line manager. As a result information collection becomes an imposition which is made worse because the person amassing the information may not know why he is collecting it. Thus in a new situation where the manager undertaking planning is trying to make new decisions (or informed decisions for the first time) the provision of information is resisted because its purpose is not understood. Secondly, even where the flow is established, the lack of commitment to providing the data may result in it being hurriedly collected with a consequent effect on its reliability.

This problem is made more difficult because the manager will be unable to predict all the decisions he wishes to make and therefore will not know with certainty what information he needs. A crucial decision today may quickly fade into insignificance tomorrow, while an aspect of the manpower situation to which previously hardly a second thought was given may be catapulted into prominence by trade union or government action. Two current examples are the employment of women and the opportunities given them, and the use of contractors — regarded by trade unionists as an extension of the 'lump'.

The manager must make an intelligent assessment of his future requirements for manpower information by anticipating changing perspectives and problems but he will have to accept a need for revision and updating. If the information system is established by the personnel or other departments as a service to management, this is a particularly delicate problem. If the system fails to meet the requests a manager makes it is liable to fall into disrepute. Consequently the needs of line managers must be sought before the information base is established. Their agreement to share in its development will be useful when the problems of maintenance and collection have to be met.

The manager (especially when he is having to provide the effort) often asks why so much information is needed. Occasionally there is a tendency to overestimate requirements and become somewhat self-indulgent about information needs. The result is to strain the patience of the provider especially if he can see the information he works to collect lying unused.

Because manpower management has become increasingly complex, the need to understand how it works becomes more necessary and more difficult. This can only be done with information that reflects the complexity of the organization's manpower. The change in society means that an organization must change its policies to take account of a changing environment. The rate of change means that the manager must regularly review what is happening. This implies a need for frequency in collecting information. Change works both ways and some information may become obsolete, just as new information will be needed. Unfortunately, once established, information returns have a remarkable capacity for continuing long after they are required. The system should include a mechanism by which obsolete items/returns can be deleted from it.

Change and the rate at which it takes place has another important effect which emphasizes the need for updated information. What the manager has experienced in the past will form the basis of his judgements in the future. Experience is highly regarded in organizations and often long service experience is a major criterion for promotion. But in an environment of rapid and significant change experience may quickly become outdated. A way of behaving and working, which in different times lasted many generations and certainly through a man's working life, may become irrelevant almost as quickly as it has become assimilated. The manager must therefore constantly check and update his experience against the known current situation. He cannot assume that, having learnt something, this knowledge will hold good in the future. This is particularly obvious in technological fields, such as the computer field where a new development can change an entire perspective, greatly affecting how a situation is dealt with.

The manager is therefore attempting to form a clear picture of the organization and the environment in which it is operating. His ability to manage the environment will depend to a large extent on the detail and accuracy of this picture, which will in turn depend on the information which helps to form it. This should not be regarded as a recommendation to collect every possible piece of information. The manager will have to identify which areas are most important and collect what information he must to cover them. In any event skilful interpretation of the information will be required if it is to mean anything; cost limitations will restrict the effort available and therefore the data that can be collected.

The manpower planning framework set out in Figure 4 indicates the coverage of information required. Information on employees is essential as well as external labour market information. To be complete the range must cover the financial and marketing aspects of the organization's operations. Having recognized this, it is helpful to work through the problems and opportunities with which the organization is faced.

In a small organization where the manager knows everyone personally, formal information requirements will be less rigorous than in large labour intensive organizations with a history of manpower problems.

Manpower review

Having put the collection of manpower information in

its organizational context, decided what sort and depth of analysis may be required and highlighted some problem areas, it is possible to start looking at information requirements on the people employed.

To repeat, information is required to make decisions: what decisions are to be influenced? There are a number of areas of manpower decision, most of which are interdependent in that a decision to recruit will affect manning levels, may result in increased training and development and can be expected to lead to more wastage especially if the recruitment programme is large. The organization may be making decisions in the following areas:

Employment levels
How many employees are required? What qualifications are needed/are we short of? Have we an age problem? Are there signs of overmanning or shortages and vacancies? Is the manpower what is needed or are changes required?

Recruitment
What employees should be recruited? Is an apprentice recruitment programme needed? Are graduates needed for managerial succession? Are we to recruit in the open market or recruit and 'grow our own'? What is the correct balance?

Wastage
Is wastage excessive and is it causing operational problems? Is it lower in some departments than others? Why are employees leaving?

Promotion
What are the promotion criteria we use? (not those explicitly stated — if any — but those used in practice). Do we promote on service and should this continue?

What sort of promotees are in the organization's best long and short term interests? Is there sufficient promotion material in the organization? What is the balance between shop floor and graduate entrant promotions? Are enough managers available for immediate and longer term requirements?

At the investigation stage it is necessary to highlight these and similar problems facing the organization. It is as well to remember that this is a static picture whereas the organization is dynamic, that is continually changing in a changing environment. Consequently the information collected at a particular time should be supplemented by information on how it is changing. Of course the flows through the manpower system are collected for a second purpose. It is through the management of flows that change is achieved. If there is a long term shortage of potential managerial talent, a recruitment programme of educated young people can be instituted. This can be backed by a suitable policy of promotion, training and career development:

FIGURE 42
Information for manpower planning

Information on jobs
Number of jobs
Whether temporary/permanent/shift/daywork/hours
Department/section
Occupation and level in organization
Skills and education and knowledge required

Information on people
Number of employees
Temporary/permanent/shift/daywork/hours
Skills and education level achieved
Grade/salary

Sex
Age
Date started (length of service)

Information on leavers
Number of leavers
Temporary/permanent/shift/daywork/hours
Date of leaving and length of service at leaving
Reason for leaving
Age on leaving
Grade/salary
Sex
Education/skills
Occupation/level in organization

Overtime and contractors/and agency staff
Overtime and contractors used
Department
Occupation
Reason

Vacancies
Number of vacancies
temporary/permanent
Department
Occupation and level
Reason for vacancy (leaver, unrequisitioned establishment etc)
Whether advertised or being advertised
Whether filled by agency staff
Length of time unfilled

Information on recruits
Number of recruits
Temporary/permanent/shift/daywork/hours

Date of starting
Age at recruitment
Grade/salary
Skill and education level
Source and method of entry
Sex
Occupation and level in organization recruited to

Information on promotions
Number of promotions
Temporary/permanent/shift/daywork/hours
Date of promotion
Reason for promotion
Grade/salary promoted from and to
Skill/education level
Sex
Age
Occupation and level in the organization promoted
from and to
Length of service

Absenteeism
Number of employees absent
Days lost
Occupation and level in the organization
Grade
Age and Sex
Length of service

The information listed in Figure 42 will give the required knowledge about employment and movements. A close study of this information will reveal many difficulties that have not been noticed and whose problems may have been shown indirectly, such as wastage. On the other hand areas will be opened up in which the organization may be able to make improvements in morale and efficiency.

A few points of advice may be helpful. The list is not comprehensive but suggests possible areas that may usefully be covered. Every list of information will be unique to the needs to a particular organization, though ththere will be some common areas. And information crucial to one organization may be irrelevant to another.

The danger should be avoided of only counting manpower directly employed: if use is made of overtime and contractors, employment levels may give a false impression of manpower utilization and costs.

Information listed here is not intended to cover everything needed to general personnel work. The record system of a personnel department may well be more detailed concerning employees though it may have less coverage on some of the other fields listed.

The updating of the information should be considered when the system is being established. Data such as age is put in once and never changed; qualifications may change infrequently while salary may fluctuate more often. The problems of updating should be thought through. If the information cannot be maintained there may be little point in collecting it except as a one-off exercise.

The codes should be simply constructed. Straightforward listing should be avoided in favour of a structured method. Figure 43 shows an organization code. The structure of the code will enable the manager more simply to integrate at different levels. Remember also that alpha codes (a, b, c etc) are more easily confused than numeric codes (0, 1, 2, 3 etc) and this may result in inaccuracies creeping into the system.

It is not necessary to code everything that is codable. An example is the education/qualification code. For

FIGURE 43
A structured organization coding

1st digit function	2nd digit department	3rd digit section	4th and 5th digit cost centre
1 Marketing	1 Domestic sales	1 Doorstep 2 Retail	10 Areas A 20 B 30 C
	2 Support	1 Marketing research 2 Advertising and publicity 3 Customer service	1 to 8 List of retail outlets for A 01 Interviewers 02 Analysts 03 Displays 04 Press and TV 05 Customer contact 06 Office administration

Therefore an employee in the Press and TV cost centre has a code of 1 (Marketing), 2 (Support), 2 (Advertising) and 14 (Area A, Press and TV). In this way the manager can easily aggregate or breakdown as required.

manpower planning purposes a general indication of education/qualification level may be sufficient (see Figure 44). Insufficient detail is provided for a personnel record and additional digits will be required for this purpose.

Finally, some of the information may not be required for individuals. Manpower planning is largely concerned with aggregates and depends on the ability to group employees into sufficiently similar groups. Where individual aspects play a more important role in decisions (for example, managerial succession planning) it may be necessary to hold information on individuals. For many other employees, aggregated information may well prove sufficient for planning purposes.

FIGURE 44
Example of Education/qualification Listing

A	Higher degree
B	Postgraduate diploma or certificate
C	First degree or certificate
D	College diploma or certificate
E	Professional qualifications equivalent to a degree
F	Other professional qualifications
G	Higher national Diploma
H	Higher national Certificate
J	GCSE/GCE 'A' Level
K	Ordinary National Diploma
L	GCSE/GCE 'O' Level
M	Technician level
N	Craftsman level
P	Operative level
Q	Royal Society of Arts
R	Other City and Guilds Awards
S	Certificates of competence, eg Masters Cert.
T	Primary
V	CSE
W	ONC
X	Other

from IMS and British Gas

Occupational classification

Aggregation will be necessary in the important area of the jobs or occupations people do. Except where only a few are employed, jobs will have to be grouped in some way. But manpower is not a homogeneous resource. People and the jobs they do are different and for planning purposes it would be foolish to work with a system that grouped labourers and managers. The degree of discrimination required in the system will depend on a number of factors. First, in principle the manager should work to separate occupations which demand different programmes of recruitment, training, remuneration and development. Secondly, if compromise is necessary (ie in the early stages a simple system may be preferred) it is a good idea to concentrate on classifying in more detail those occupations which are most important to the organization.

The problem of classifying jobs should not be treated lightly. In many ways it is crucial to the information system and, if the method is not adequate, use of the system will be more difficult.

Much effort has been put into occupation classification by various organizations, government bodies and research organizations.

The traditional approach to classifying jobs has been one which used job titles. The method simply listed all the job titles in the organization, perhaps resolving areas of extreme duplication or overlap, and in more sophisticated efforts attempted to give the list an element of structure.

This approach is not wholly satisfactory for organizations who are aware of the increasing importance of manpower management and the need for an adequate classification system. The system is important because fundamentally in manpower planning we are concerned with what people do. All the effort is directed towards ensuring that certain tasks are undertaken as required by the organization to meet its corporate objectives. It is essential that if planning is to be done well there must be a language which adequately describes the jobs. The Manpower Society along with the IMS was among the first to recognize the problem (reference 45).

An example is given in a review of England in the year 1067. The working population of Norman England at that time was one million and a half and if you look at the manpower structure, this is what you find: the position two and a half months after the Battle of Hastings and exactly one week after William was crowned in Westminster Abbey.

Manpower analysis of Norman England 1.1.1067

King	1
Earls	a few
Barons	180
Lords of the Manor	1,000
Freemen	250,000
Villeins	550,000
Bordars and Cottars	475,000
Slaves	125,000
Ecclesiastics	20,000
Merchants	1,000
Butchers and bakers	4,000
Bow and arrow makers	10,000
Potters	10,000
Jouneymen and labourers	60,000

1,506,181
+ a few earls

This list shows the characteristic activities of the time. If you study it, one thing strikes you immediately.

You can easily visualize an activity of bow and arrow making. Similarly it is not difficult to visualize an activity of slaving or peasanting or an activity of pottering — making pots. These are things you do.

On the other hand, you don't do Kinging or Earling, nor for that matter do you do baroning. These are not so much things that you do as things that you are,

167

although no doubt there were certain duties associated with these particular types of people.

Looking at it another way, you could easily visualize that the king might or might not be wicked or that Barons might or might not be wicked (they usually were). On the other hand the concept of a wicked bow and arrow maker or a wicked pot maker comes much less easily to mind. The capacity for being wicked is clearly related to a person's position in the hierarchy. In fact the list mixes up the concepts of activity (the jobs people do) with authority (where people are in the hierarchy).

This same problem exists in the job titles used in organizations today.

When considering a list of job titles, the problem of using them for occupational classification will become apparent:

chairman
chief accountant
clerk
engine fitter
chargehand engine fitter

These are the kinds of activities which most organizations will have and which our manpower strategies are designed to achieve. It is not difficult to imagine an activity such as 'clerking' or 'engine fitting' but the addition of 'chargehand' to engine fitting begins to describe the job in different terms. A chargehand is less a description of what one does and is more a description of what one is. It begins to describe hierarchical status in the organization. This is accentuated in the position of 'chairman'. That term carries no indication of activity but is a statement of seniority in the organization, an indication of authority. 'Chief accountant' describes both the activity of the job (accounting) and the level in the organization at which it is carried out (chief).

Any list of job titles conveys a range of information such as activity and authority, together with an implication of the level of ability and knowledge required to do the job. These concepts are indiscriminately mixed. From a managerial point of view this is a weakness. Sometimes it will be necessary to extract the various pieces of information and use them in various ways. A list of job titles cannot be broken down because the various concepts are already lost in the overall job title.

Two major systems were developed to deal with this problem. These were CODOT (common occupation directory of job titles), which was developed by the Department of Employment, and IMSSOC (Institute of Manpower Studies System of Occupational Classification). Of these IMSSOC was the more sophisticated, but it suffered from being not practical enough and its implementation proved fraught.

The effort of implementing and, perhaps even more, updating such a system was underestimated by those firms who attempted the task. If there is a system of job evaluation backed by job descriptions it is less of a problem, but each occupation in the organization has to be looked at and carefully classified.

The relative failure to solve the problem of classification is not to say that the research effort was wasted, though a personnel manager is unlikely to find another firm recommending anything other than its own home-grown occupation coding system.

If the organization has an established system of classifying jobs, it is best retained and refined. CODOT is a good example of a system that works for its user but is of limited value in a company. The conclusion is that an economy-wide employment system of classification is not feasible. The company is best advised to live with its own occupation titles and build on them.

External manpower environment
In the chapter on manpower supply reference was made to the lack of information and understanding concerning the external environment. This is partly because the complex factors influencing labour supply make it difficult to grasp them all. Also the manager would normally gain more benefit from studying the organization's internal manpower environment before looking outside; many early efforts have therefore concentrated there. As a result, it is easier to specify what information is required than to find the information itself so it can be analysed. Some of the information to which the organization should refer is listed in Figure 45. Most information will be required at the level at which the firm operates — national, regional or local. Unfortunately it is often necessary to make do with information not relating directly to the labour market from which the firm draws its labour. Nevertheless the manager should be able to receive help and advice from the DE and the IMS to ensure an intelligent interpretation of the information available.

FIGURE 45
External manpower information

Education trends and forecasts
School leavers
GCSE and A level certificate leavers
Supply from technical colleges by subject
Supply of graduates by subject
Future trends

Labour market (national/regional/local)
Total in market
Age
Sex
Growth/decline in market
Occupation
Shortages and surpluses

Unemployment
Total unemployed (and short time working)
Sex
Age
Length of time unemployed
Occupation

Employers in area
Activity of competing employers
Growth/contraction of major firms
Occupations surplus/in demand
Future plans
Labour/capital intensive

Migration
Employees moving from/to other areas
Availability of employees in other areas
Age
Sex
Occupation

Economic and political
Plans for the region
Level of economic activity regionally/locally
National economic trends
Government policy
Investment grant availability
Grant availability for expansion

Marketing and financial information
Figure 4 illustrated the framework for manpower planning and referred to the need to consider the marketing and financial objectives of the organization. This area is particularly crucial because it is probably the main single determinant of manpower requirements; also, many organizations are judged by their performance here.

FIGURE 46
Marketing and financial

Capital investment plan
Automation plans
Sales campaign — types of sales
Market strategies
Centralization/decentralization
Acquisition and merger and selling off
Product diversification
Financial and profit targets
Competitor position

When preparing his manpower plans, the manager should be looking at the various aspects listed in Figure 46.

Utilization, productivity and working practices
The poor state of productivity performance of many British firms is a major reason for attaching greater efforts to manpower management. It is essential that the investigation stage highlights the organization's problems of utilization, productivity and working practices. The measurement of labour productivity is concerned with expressing:

$$\frac{numbers\ employed}{output}$$

172

This was used as a basis for forecasting and analysing manpower demand in an earlier chapter. If the manager wishes to pursue this subject he should refer to an International Labour Office Publication, *Measuring Labour Productivity*[39] (see Figure 47 for the table of factors suggested).

FIGURE 47
Factors influencing labour productivity

Human factors
Labour-management relations
Social and psychological conditions of work
Wage incentives
Adaptability to, and liking for, the job
Physical fatigue
Composition (age, sex, skill and training) for the labour
   force
Organization of the spirit of emulation in production
Trade union practices

Organization and technical factors
Degree of integration
Percentage of capacity used
Size and stability of production
Quality of raw materials
Adequate and even flow of materials
Subdivision of operations
Balancing of equipment
Multiple machine systems
Control devices
Quality of output
Rationalization and standardization of work and
   material
Layout and location of the plant
Maintenance and engineering service: safety, light,
   sound, ventilation, air conditioning, telephone etc

173

Availability, fitness and accessibility of tools
Wear and tear of machines and tools
Amount of machinery (or power) available per worker
Proportion of maintenance labour to operating labour
Length and distribution of working hours
Selection of personnel

General factors
Climate
Geographical distribution of raw materials
Fiscal and credit policies
General organization of the labour market
Proportion of the labour force to the total population, degree of unemployment, of labour shortage, of labour turnover
Technical centres and information concerning new techniques
Commercial organization and size of market
General scientific and technical research
Variations in the composition of the output
Influence of low-efficiency plants and their varying proportion in total output

Source
International Labour Office, 1969, *Measuring Labour Productivity*

It is often difficult to relate a given output with a given group of employees; in these circumstances different ways of measuring performance are required. One method is to relate manpower used to its cost; and the managerial judgements have to be made as to whether the cost incurred is acceptable in view of the result obtained.

An alternative method can be used where different plants, offices or other separable units are available for measurement. Manning at one can be compared with manning at another and weaknesses highlighted and dealt with.

Individual departmental objectives can be set and criteria established by which success can be judged. This is useful where individual jobs are concerned.

A remarkable example of how to measure productivity simply and effectively is given by R J Howard at the IPM's Manpower Planning in Practice Course.

By the simple device of noting the power consumed by machinery in a plant a compelling point is made. This is shown in Figure 48. Without a full knowledge of the nature of the plant and its operations it is important not to overstate what the graph may show. Nevertheless in one chart there is a good measure of productivity and some difficult questions to be faced by management and employees. It would be interesting to note trade union or management reaction to the disclosure of this

FIGURE 48
Power consumption graph

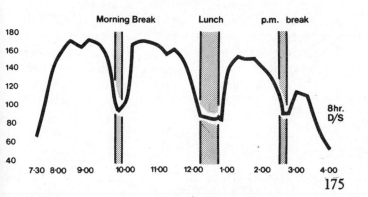

sort of information within the organization. To disclose it to the public or to shareholders may be more than many could stand. This is the sort of simple presentation that is needed. The message of productivity is so often lost in weighty reports produced by specialist departments which are long past giving of their best. The idea given here is also included in Purkiss[19] in greater detail and with more mathematical support.

Finally reference should be made to the working practices of the organization. Many may well restrain progress. The manager will not underestimate the difficulty of removing old practices or replacing them.

To conclude this chapter it may be helpful to set out the problems in collecting information.

Problems in collecting information
lack of information hinders good management
information is for decisions — which decisions does the
    organization wish to make?
avoid asking for too much information, it is better to
    understate the need
different levels of detail are needed
how will new information be added and old deleted?
gain managerial support; crucial for collection and
    maintenance

It is worth noting that information is the very stuff of manpower planning. Indeed this chapter could well have been the first in this book. On the other hand there is a tendency to become bogged down by the mechanics and the reasons for collecting information is lost. This must be avoided and is a lesson relevant to the next chapter on computers and models.

9 Computers and models in manpower planning

Much of the early interest in manpower planning arose from the application of computing and operational research techniques to the manpower field. To some extent the development of theory went ahead of practical application. Many managers found the techniques difficult to understand and could see little that would help them in solving their manpower problems. A tendency to dismiss the application of computers and models to personnel management followed, as being wholly inappropriate. Fortunately it seems that the worst excesses of that tendency have been avoided. This chapter sets out the general principles as they have developed so far. It suggests practical ways in which the manager could make progress by looking first at computerizing personnel information and then at exploiting that information base through models.

Should it be computerized?
It is usual and tempting to present the manager with a table showing the sort of record and information systems required related to the number of employees in the organization. Manual systems are thus recommended where there are only a few hundred employees and computers where there are a few thousand. Such advice may have been appropriate previously but not now.

177

There are two reasons: first, the increasing availability of computing devices makes it easy to justify the use of computers for personnel management. The existence of computer bureaux means that the manager need be involved in limited costs while the development of fast retrieval devices makes the effort worthwhile. Secondly, a great deal will depend on the complexity of the manpower system that is being managed. An organization that requires highly educated and finely balanced teams of technical managers may well find its succession and development problems greatly helped by the use of computer and model techniques. Big problems needing the help of computers do not only come from big numbers.

In any event, the availability of inexpensive computing power means that the question on computers is one of 'which' not 'whether'. The decision will also be influenced by the availability of computing facilities, either through a bureau or through the organization's own facilities. The way in which the payroll is handled may also affect decisions: if it is computerized substantial use may be made of the information it holds for manpower planning. Even where the payroll is undertaken by an outside agency, it may be possible to come to an arrangement on access for manpower planning. If it is due for revision a manpower information system may be included. It is important that the manager should keep in touch with payroll developments so that he can add his own needs to the system specification. Finally, after costs, the need for the system should be the determining factor on whether to computerize. Where manpower is well managed by a professional staff capable of handling by computer the problems the organization faces, it is sensible to provide the necessary facilities. Where a computerized system would not be properly exploited it may be unwise to provide it.

It is worth reminding ourselves of the problems computers can bring when well-meaning experts construct a system far more complex than that required and far in advance of a manager's need or ability to use it. This is shown pictorially in Figure 49 in the apocryphal story of the poor line manager whose attempt to have a simple swing was taken over by the experts. It happens easily and the reader is warned to be on his guard. If the personnel function is expected to carry the resposnibility for the result, then the computerized personnel system should be managed by that function.

Relationship with payroll

When a decision has been taken to computerize the company's manpower information system, its relationship with the payroll must be made clear. Either links or integration is a must.

A main reason for integrating personnel and payroll systems is that the payroll can always exert its short-term priorities over other systems. If the systems are separate, short term pressure will increase the accuracy of the payroll whereas there will be less pressure to maintain the accuracy of the personnel system. When the systems are integrated this disadvantage should be reversed and work in favour of the personnel system.

There are sensible practical reasons in favour of integration. Much documentation required for both systems is common and saves wasted clerical effort. For example, similar documents are required for new starters to ensure they are paid and that a personal file is raised: it is unnecessarily wasteful to have two documents, and even worse two clerks, and finally two separate inputs to the computer. Also duplication of files of common information means that not only are documents duplicated but updating cycles are too.

There are likely to be practical problems in meeting

FIGURE 49
A computer system

1 As management requested it

2 As the project leader defined it

3 As systems designed it

4 As programming developed it

5 As operations installed it

6 What the user wanted

this ideal. Usually the payroll and personnel departments will be separated organizationally and there may be a limited history of cooperation. Through its negotiations with trade unions, the personnel function affects pay systems more than any other department. Rates of pay, hours and premiums, shift work, special allowances and even the date and speed at which wages are paid are coming within the ambit of negotiation. The finance function is consequently tending to be isolated from the decisions that affect the system it manages. When pay circulations are processed within the computer the finance function really becomes the cashier, and bank giro and use of security firms for paying wages make that role less important, although there are now frequent examples of organizations which have located the payroll within the personnel function. With so many systems dealing with tax and insurance that can

180

be 'bought in' from software houses, this area is not the problem it once was.

Where the personnel system covers information more specifically needed for manpower management, integration may be a better prospect than in situations where a vast personnel system covering all employee personal information is being considered.

Information to be included and problems of updating and confidentiality

It is possible to include every piece of information that would conceivably be of any use but a selection will be more likely. It is a good discipline to define the need for each piece of information. In practice it will probably be found necessary to balance the 'nice to have information' with the 'what I will really need' information. The personnel manager should not forget to consult functional management about their needs as well as clearly establishing his own.

The complexity of the final system is important. For quite sophisticated manpower planning, only limited information is required (see chapter 8) whereas much greater detail will be needed if the system is intended to replace manual records completely. The system will have to be flexible so that further information can be added if necessary. Detailed analysis of what might be included was considered in chapter 8.

The cost of establishing and then maintaining the information is important. The information can be so complex that maintenance costs or maintenance problems become prohibitive.

The availability of information will need to be considered. It might be desirable for instance to have information on 'reasons for leaving', including such reasons as 'personal relation problems' and 'more money'. If such information is likely to be of spurious accuracy it is

181

better left out. Only information that is readily available and can be expected to be accurate should be stored.

A decision will have to be made about history, that is, information about previous employees or 'old' information of present employees. Some history will be required in the system: a rough guide is to provide the same number of years of history as one expects to forecast using it. Some selectivity in storing historical information will probably be required. Some may be kept indefinitely and some deleted immediately new information makes it obsolete. Storing information, especially 'on-line', can be expensive but it is possible to hold only present information on disc files and transfer history to tape, which reduces storage costs. But access to the information then becomes less easy and thus it is more difficult to use, though some bureaux appear to have overcome this problem to some extent.

The confidential aspects of file content are another consideration. Some information may be considered too confidential and too private for inclusion. Whether the emotive attitude to storing personal information in computers will fade with time as their use becomes widespread and accepted is a possibility. Efforts should be concentrated on file security rather than on not including confidential information.

Updating the system is liable to be difficult. If the system is integrated with payroll, updating will be less difficult, especially if the information directly affects remuneration. In general there will be a direct relationship between the type of information included and problems of updating. Personal information can be updated by providing employees at intervals with a print-out of information about themselves to update and return. This method has the added advantage of allaying fears that employees may have about file content. Of course, Data Protection legislation in the UK and other countries now ensures that a responsible view is taken towards accuracy and disclosure.

Separating job and person files

The literature on computer applications to personnel work does not seem to bring out the possibility of separating jobs and man files. This has been a major feature of the gas industry's Personnel Management Information System (PMIS) (see Figure 50). It involves identifying information which relates to the job itself such as grade, qualifications and experience required, and also identifying information relating to individual employees.

FIGURE 50
Personnel management information system
A total concept

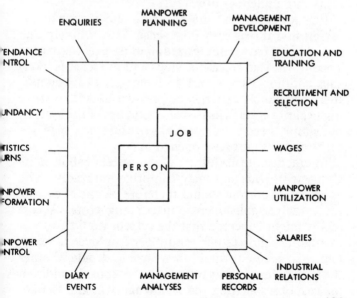

Such separation between people and jobs has the advantage of making it possible to undertake a matching of jobs and people to identify areas of imbalance. It may be useful to know how many professionally qualified people are in jobs where their qualifications are not required, especially if there is a shortage of employees with such qualifications in another department.

Costing the system

Various attempts have been made at cost benefit analysis in the computer field but success has been patchy in this country, as it has elsewhere.

In the USA attempts have been made to undertake comprehensive costs analyses. The costs of the present system are fully investigated and the costs of the new system compared with them but the savings have been difficult to pin down when, like many statistics, they evaporate under scrutiny.

It is arguable that the object should not be a cost saving in a direct cash flow sense. It is unlikely that straightforward computerization of an existing record system will lead to cash savings and in fact it is likely that additional costs will be incurred. For example, there will almost certainly be pressure to employ more high calibre specialists to make good use of the system, not simply because it exists but because new management opportunities are opened up.

In practice the usefulness of the system will lie in its ability to provide and analyse information readily. The approach to costing should therefore be one of costing the initial establishment and running costs. A cost report might conclude that the system would cost x£s to establish and x£s per annum per employee to maintain. Management would then have to decide whether the facility for analysis was worth that sum. In addition the cost of installation and maintenance might usefully be related to the firm's payroll costs, in comparison with which they will be small.

Input and retrieval devices

Even where payroll and personnel systems are not integrated it should be possible to have common input documents simultaneously updating files. Documentation within the organization will call for a special system study to eliminate duplication and reduce errors. Unfortunately many computer systems (not just for personnel/payroll) have been implemented without adequate advance systems study by a professional organization and methods department.

Throughout the design of the system a careful watch will have to be kept on the ease with which information can be extracted. It is not uncommon to find that particular information cannot be retrieved without extensive and costly programming. Increasing technical exploitation of computers will help. In the longer term such hardware peripherals will become cheaper and more easily justified.

The needs of units which do not operate at a central point will require attention: it should be possible to provide separate locations with information in any of two forms. First, it is technically feasible and increasingly inexpensive to provide terminal facilities so that the outlying districts can interrogate the main system. A second approach is to provide standard listings on a regular basis backed by a rapid enquiry service with an effective and speedy turnround.

The final consideration on the type of retrieval devices installed will depend on how the system is to be used. The choices are standard pre-set listings, *ad hoc* requests using a generalized reporting system, visual display units (VDU) and remote terminals. Added to these can be useful devices such as telephone links and graph plotters.

The manager may be reluctant to tolerate a system which is slower than his present manual one. Despite the speed at which computers work, without adequate retrieval facilities information cannot be easily extracted. This ironical situation is now eased by the availability of standard interrogation packages which the manager with no special computing and programming ability can use. Nevertheless the system will not be as flexible as that provided by manual records for individual record enquiries. A computer system serves when dealing with complex aggregation such as in planning. The personnel manager may find it difficult to justify immediate random access to the files, so most requests should be provided through predetermined standard listings. There is no reason (except perhaps cost) why information cannot be provided in the form of record cards printed by the computer directly on to continuous stationery. For routine questions such an approach is satisfactory and will ensure as rapid a response to a question as with a manual system.

It is not always possible to predetermine information needs in this way. The manager is often exploring a situation and his next question is only known when he has seen the answer to the last.

The computer provides this important facility for progressive analysis and discovery in uncertain situations and it is a waste of its power to restrict it to routine questions and answers. This is the answer to management services specialists who try to save money by arguing that you will only have to wait 24 hours and is that not quick enough? This attitude is a misconception of how people actually work. The manager needs to carry on a 'conversation' with the computer and perhaps with his colleagues. This is an argument for making terminal facilities available to the manager. Imagine the difficulty in trying to carry on a discussion with someone who replied to each question 12 hours later! It might be sufficient in simple question and answer situations (how many engine fitters do we employ?) but it would limit intelligent and creative investigation of an undefined manpower problem.

This sort of retrieval device moves the manager into the field of manpower modelling.

Manpower models

Much of the interest in manpower planning in the later 1960s centred on the application to manpower problems of manpower models. A great deal of ignorance and mystique surrounds manpower modelling; the purpose of this section is to provide an introduction to the subject as it relates to manpower planning in the organization. It is not concerned with models generally which may have application in manpower planning, such as with models of workload from which forecasts of manpower requirements can be derived. These were referred to in chapter 3. The inter-disciplinary nature of manpower planning allows many different types of techniques to be used by specialists from a variety of backgrounds and it would be inappropriate to go into them all here. This chapter describes models of an organization's manpower system. The majority of such models relate to analysing and planning manpower supply though they can also be used in identifying manpower required.

What is a manpower model?

A model is usually thought of as a mathematical representation of the relationships in a manpower system. The representation is usually in the form of mathematical equations, which are themselves a condensed lan-

187

guage expressing what is occurring. It helps to begin by thinking of manpower as a system. An example of a simple manpower system is shown in Figure 51. The rectangle represents a group of employees known as 'stocks' and the arrows represent movements into and out of and within the system known as 'flows'. The use of jargon such as 'stocks' and 'flows' may well be appropriate among managers who need a condensed language to avoid the necessity for having to refer to

FIGURE 51

Simple Manpower System

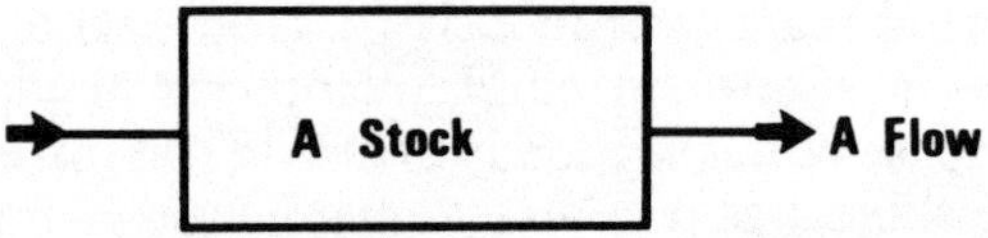
A Stock
A Flow

Complex Manpower System

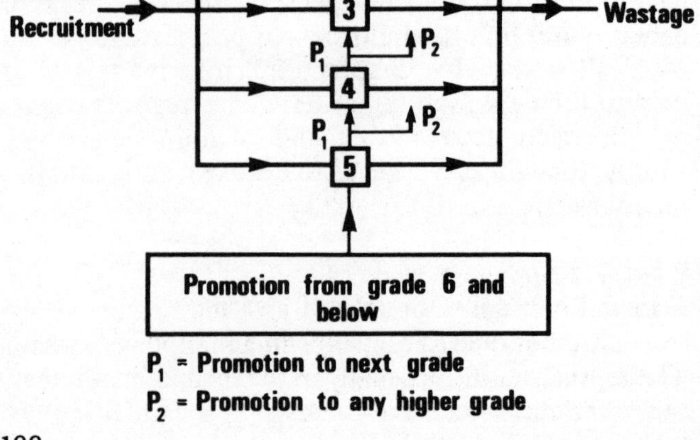
1
2
3
4
5
P1
P2
External
Recruitment
Wastage
Promotion from grade 6 and below
P1 = Promotion to next grade
P2 = Promotion to any higher grade

recruitment, wastage, promotions etc., but those unused to such terminology may get the impression of a mechanistic approach to human problems: consequently unwitting offence may be given.

In practice the manpower system will be considerably more complex than the one shown here and will look more like the system also in Figure 51, which represents an organization's management structure. Sub-systems often can and should be identified so it becomes necessary to distinguish within the system by age, length of service or by department and section. The result is what in practice managers are faced with — an exceedingly complex dynamic system of inter-relationships. Even if the flows were stable (which they never are) the people themselves are continually changing and changing the jobs as a result. Because the manpower system is complex, the manager needs help in understanding and managing it. This is the purpose of a model. In a complex system the boxes can be given mathematical symbols to facilitate computation. This is how systems are often presented in manpower textbooks.

Types and uses of manpower models
Models are often classified as being 'stochastic' or 'deterministic'. A deterministic model is one which represents events in fixed terms. It says, for instance, that the organization will employ 25 engineers in five years' time. A stochastic model is not concerned with fixed values and events but with the probability appertaining to a value or event. It thus expresses the future in terms of the likelihood of an event occuring: for example the organization is most likely to be employing 25 engineers in five years' time but there is a slightly lower probability that it will employ 24 and lower still 23. It is possible to assign probabilities to individual

189

forecasts so that the manager can consider the degree of certainty with which he is dealing. In a situation of complexity and doubt, the stochastic model is likely to give a more realistic assessment of the future. The manager has to discover by practice whether the additional sophistication of the system is worth the mathematical complexity involved.

Models may be used in three inter-related ways. First, they can be used to gain an awareness of how the present manpower system works: investigation allows the manager to test the effect of wastage on promotion opportunities or of recruitment on numbers in post, for example. Secondly, the model can be used for prediction.

By finding regularities in past events they can be projected into the future and an indication of what might happen under certain conditions ascertained. Thirdly, the model can be used for planning. By specifying and changing relationships between stocks and flows it allows the manager to investigate the possible or likely consequences in terms of manpower strategies, and to test the effect of his proposed policies for recruitment and promotion before he finally decides whether to put them into practice. He can for instance determine whether a reduction in external recruitment will have the hoped-for effect on the promotion prospects of the people he employs.

This planning capacity is often used to plan strategies designed to achieve manpower requirements. It is possible to use the model to design the structure of the system that determines what manpower is required. An example would be looking at the effects of changing the relationship between managers, supervisors and craftsmen. The manager can look at a variety of options and decide which would best suit the needs of the organization. The recruitment, promotion and training programmes required to meet it can then be worked out.

Markov and renewal models

Two major manpower models are in common usage. Their development owes a great deal to Professor Bartholomew's efforts while at the University of Kent at Canterbury. Much of the detailed development was undertaken within the Civil Service Department and much of the responsibility for drawing the principles into an applicable framework belongs to Andrew Forbes. The development of the suite of manpower planning models has continued at IMS from whom further information and advice is available.

Markov models start with a given group of employees and, given the flows in (eg recruitment and promotions from outside the system) and the flows out (eg wastage and promotion to outside the system), they estimate the likely numbers of employees in the future. This type of model is particularly useful where knowledge exists about present employees and the likely flows over succeeding years, but where the required manpower in the future is not known. Many of the models in this group should be referred to as Markov type models, as the full so-called Markov chain model requires future movements to be expressed in terms of probabilities such as the probably wastage or promotion from each of the categories. The Markov model is based on the assumption that future employees in any grade are determined to so much by the numbers required in that grade but by promotions and recruitment encouraging movement up through the system. Because of this 'pushing' effect of recruitment and promotions, Markov models are often referred as to as 'push' models.

In practice the numbers in the post may not be free to change to meet the effect of recruitment and promotion but are more likely to be constrained within fairly narrow limits of manpower requirements. The future manpower strength is known: what is required is knowledge of how much recruitment and how many promotions should take place to meet it. Consequently the basic assumption of a renewal model is that requirements are met by changes in promotions and recruitment rates. In this way employees are 'pulled' through the system to meet predetermined requirements. Renewal models are therefore often called 'pull' models. They are particularly useful where future manpower requirements are known within reasonable limits and what flows are required to meet them must be determined.

In many organizations the 'push' and 'pull' effects are probably working at the same time. Perhaps promotions are taking place because of past expectations with limited concern for the consequent effect on grade sizes (push) or employees are promoted (or not promoted) solely on a predetermined manpower need (pull). 'Push-pull' models have consequently been developed, allowing the manager to use both effects at once. The use of models as a prediction and planning tool should be stressed, since they enable quite complex manpower organizations to be studied by the manager. All the calculations undertaken by the model can in theory be done with a desk calculator but the time taken would be prohibitive. The availability of computers have made this type of planning using models possible.

Criticisms of manpower models
The first and most often heard criticism of modelling in the personnel field is that it dehumanizes the individual. The argument runs that, reduced to numbers (to 'stocks' and 'flows'), the individual's liberty and integrity is somehow threatened. It would be unwise to
192

dismiss this argument as simply reaction to any new development. The manager must be aware of the assumptions that underlie the model and recognize their limitations: models are an aid to decision making and cannot make decisions; also there will be many areas that the model is not capable of representing and where the manager must therefore make a judgement.

The best models do not seek to limit human behaviour. On the contrary, the expression of probabilities is a recognition of the inherent variability in human behaviour, in which nevertheless tendency and similarity can be found when aggregates are considered.

A second criticism is that the theoretical study of model building has run far ahead of practical application and the data available. Professor Bartholomew writes:

> There is considerable truth in this criticism, but I think it puts the cart before the horse. It presupposes that data collection generates the need for methods of analysis. This I suspect is rarely the case. More often data is collected to satisfy some particular demand and hence until manpower planners specify what data they need, none will be available. The practical value of advanced model building is that it creates a blue-print for the kind of data which is necessary for effective manpower planning.[7a]

A third criticism related to the first is that manpower models are unrealistic and oversimplified. This is almost always true: it would be impossible to represent all the qualitative and quantitative factors existing within a manpower system. It is part of the model builder's art to extract the important parts of the system and represent that within his equation. It is not enough to say that a part of the system is missing: it must be

193

shown that the omission matters and affects the validity of results; for example, a manager criticized a model in general use within an organization because it did not allow for demotions. It was pointed out that the number of demotions each year were an insignificant 5 to 10 out of a total of some 800 movements. The operational researcher who had built the model had quite rightly excluded a movement that existed but whose inclusion would have created additional complexity to no overall benefit.

The manager will be aware that his own judgements, assumptions and decisions about the system are considerably simplified. The manager, perhaps, less than a model, is able to grasp the subtle and complex interrelationships within the system. But the final protection against unrealistic assumptions lies with the manager since he makes the decision. This means that he must be fully aware of the assumptions that are made within the model: he cannot leave its construction entirely to backroom specialists.

10 Future developments in manpower planning

In a sense this whole book has been about future developments in manpower planning. Despite its emphasis on practical application it has nevertheless moved into areas that for many organizations are not currently common practice.

Manpower planning and the personnel function

One point worth making is that manpower planning has managed to survive the disillusion that follows the euphoria associated with all panaceas. Manpower planning is not a panacea and in the end may not even be a distinguishable activity within itself.

The idea of the personnel function as a serving non-executive function is changing. It will certainly service the organization but, like the finance function, will exert executive powers for better manpower management. One can then envisage that manpower planning will not be an entity separate from a personnel function involved in strategic manpower matters.

The personnel function is the function closest to the organization's most volatile resource — the only resource that has quite literally a mind of its own.

One might expect the personnel function to develop new skills to meet this situation, such as technical skills of modelling, computing, statistics and behavioural sciences. The activities of operational research or computer departments would not be replaced but the personnel function would be able to develop some of its own skills.

It is particularly interesting that manpower planning became famous (some would say infamous) through quantative applications. The Manpower Society grew from a study group of the Operational Research Society and it was some years before the established personnel profession recognized that the activity existed. The early exponents of the numerate side of manpower planning were then enthusiastic that personnel management should be involved, probably because it was recognized that manpower needed a champion within the organization who was seen to be associated with it. It only needed the personnel manager to show a willingness to accept the challenge. The indications are that he has done so and that this trend will continue.

Computerization

Another development will probably lie in the use of computers in manpower problems. A generation of young managers is maturing which does not see computers as overgrown calculating machines. There are immensely complicated manpower systems that are not and probably will not be grasped without the analytic power of a computer. How this development is to take place without greater loss of human dignity than is already suffered by the individual in industry is a problem that must be tackled.

Costing and assets in manpower

This may be an area that has yet to get off the ground. It is some years since the Manpower Society working party on manpower costs reported. There is a conflict between economic and human interest in the organization. It is possible to mitigate the effect of economic and financial policies on people by good manpower policies, but this is only mitigation. Until the economic interest takes proper account of the social interest this difficulty will continue and employees and managers will argue and counter-argue that the balance is wrong. Perhaps the real breakthrough could be the new recognition of manpower not as a cost but as an asset — not as a loss maker, but as an income generator.

Behavioural science

Probably the weakest area of much of man management follows from our profound ignorance of what really leads to individual human behaviour. Progress has been made, for example, in labour turnover and the withdrawal from work concept, but the rate of application is still limited. The fact remains that people remain as ubiquitous and contrary as ever they were. We must not expect breakthroughs in the social sciences as profound as have been seen in the physical sciences.

Demand forecasting

As manpower planning becomes more integrated into overall business management, it is to be hoped that more reliable demand forecasting will result. However manpower planning is not a forecasting problem: many organizations would experience great difficulty in determining requirements in the present, let alone the future, because of an underlying assumption that the present way of organizing work into a certain range of jobs is unchangeable. The idea that a manager will ever reliably foretell the future must surely be illusory. The solution is to find what can be found and then build the flexibility into the organization to enable events to be adapted to.

Supply forecasting

Methods are available for dealing with wastage and application of the more simple techniques is what is wanted. Managers could hope for a clearer understanding of the process involved in promotions. In many areas what is needed is time to apply existing methodology.

National manpower planning

Little progress has taken place on national manpower planning. An important prerequisite of national manpower planning is a good information base. The Department of Employment/Manpower Society Report set out a framework, and this provides the necessary starting point. Organizations must be willing to provide the input to such a system.

The availability of information will help many other departments. Better labour market intelligence will indicate where firms can usefully go for labour. Better identification of training needs will ease shortages and consequent bottlenecks.

A national manpower strategy occurred — not some grand national plan, but a more flexible cohesive framework which enables managers to make more sensible manpower decisions. The recognition of the state as a provider of framework plans has been an important move forward. Productivity in manpower has increased in the 1980s, when old-fashioned central and mechanistic planning declined. Of course the spur was economic necessity not social justice!

Manpower control and corporate planning

Other important developments could come in manpower control, where sensible application would provide purpose to much wasted planning. The integration of manpower within corporate strategy-making can be expected to continue, though perhaps without manpower planning becoming part of corporate planning activity.

Trade unions

Manpower planning was bound to be affected by the decline of trade unions as a force in strategic organizational decision-taking. The disclosure of information and more open management styles is a limited step but one that will lead to employee not trade union involvement in decision-making. The emphasis, therefore, will be on employees not trade unions.

Employees, commitment and excellence

In principle, the idea of involving employees more in the decisions affecting the organization is attractive, but the problems of achieving anything meaningful are enormous. Involvement at the strategic level may be one approach, but experience shows that having a narrow self-interested group in the decision-making machinery, particularly at such an important level, is not a popular or helpful prospect. The movement of trade unions in this area was pre-empted by the more open system of management. Opportunities for individual creativity and decision-making were increased. No good was likely to come from any politically motivated move, and experience proved this. So now the search is on for the committed and flexible employee. This is where the future lies — in the search for excellence.

The flexible firm

This leads naturally to the concept of employees as the

199

creative driving force in organizations. The view that a mechanistic approach can never solve manpower problems is now accepted more readily than it was. With the emergence of a fuller understanding of the nature of strategic personnel management, everything from reward structures, job descriptions, training to competence standards not qualifications, employee relations and the rest is being rethought. It is in flexibility that the problems of the future can be overcome. For this reason flexibility has always been the foundation of good manpower planning and therefore true strategic thinking.

Finally, let us return to the personnel function itself. It is important that it has the credibility necessary to do the job it is setting itself. This involves training and development of personnel staff themselves. It is important that manpower planning skills are integrated into the personnel function and that the right calibre of staff is recruited to exercise them.

So far the twentieth century has witnessed an explosion of scientific and technological knowledge but the outstanding technical achievements have not been matched by a deeper understanding of the human condition. Whatever progress has been made, probably only the surface has been scratched when it comes to discovering how to release the creativity of people in industry. Perhaps industrial organizations are such that it is not possible. Because of astonishing failures in handling human factors in industry when compared with technical achievements, it is important that proposals and progress are made steadily and with humility. Manpower planning can probably bring benefit to manpower management in many organizations if it is carefully integrated with existing practices but it can be oversold. In the longer term, it is to be hoped that manpower planning is simply part of an increasing awareness of human need which is reflected in many growing personnel activities.

11 Conclusion

Manpower planning as it has been described here is concerned with trying to establish a clearer relationship between the work to be done and the people available to do it, not only in the present but also as far into the future as is appropriate.

Manpower planning represents much more that making a few calculations of manning and recruitment levels. Its range of activities is broad and while the personnel function and the line manager is seen as playing a leading role, it is not surprising that management services and corporate planning have a high degree of involvement. Manpower planning is *par excellence* and inter-disciplinary activity.

No 'plan' in any fixed sense will be relevant for long. In practice manpower planning is an approach to managing people at work, the benefits of which should accrue to them as well as to the organization. It is not a process by which the future is foretold. It is not like the football pools where failure results when you do not get it right. In the volatile and complex climate in which manpower is managed the unforeseen will arise. The success of manpower planning will be judged by how well the organization can anticipate or adapt to the unforeseen.

The manager cannot choose not to do manpower planning. Decisions are made and events occur. His choice is rather how much he intends to be the master or the victim of those events.

A great deal will depend on the efforts of the personnel manager. As Professor John Morris wrote in his IPM book, *Developing Resourceful Managers,* "There is a clear need for personnel managers to recognize that they are not just doing a straightforward no-nonsense job but are at a point of inter-section of some of the most important human issues of the organization. The phrase 'point of intersection' is itself too cool. 'Arena' may not be too strong a term, though many personnel managers would prefer forum". What are his priorities? They will differ depending on the organization in which he is employed but some general prinicples might be:

1 What are the organization's problems and how does manpower contribute to them both in helping and hindering?
2 Are requirements systematically identified and reviewed? What criterial if any are used? Are they appropriate?
3 Is there an adequate manpower reporting procedure with opportunites for discussing the implications? Does it cover movements (wastage, recruitment and promotions) as well as employees?
4 Does the information base need overhauling? Can more use be made of it, eg age and succession analysis?
5 Are all parts of the personnel function involved?
6 Are models, computers and statistics appropriate to help solve manpower problems? Perhaps greater use can be made of existing facilities such as payroll.
7 Is there an officer to keep abreast of manpower problems and methods both within and outside the firm? Is he skilled at his job? Has he access to

information? Consider using the IPM, the Manpower Society, the Institute of Manpower Studies and the Department of Employment.

8 Is there a programme for implementing manpower planning? Can the support of line management and senior executives be gained? What are their problems?

9 Manpower reports should deal with these problems and should be short and to the point (backed by detailed study but not presented to management unless they ask for it).

10 What are the costs and benefits to the organization and the employee?

Tackling these principles should keep most organizations occupied. It is a difficult task for the personnel manager, who must be competent to harmonize such different approaches. It is hoped that this text will have been useful to him and to the line manager in selecting priorities and methods. If so, the point made at the beginning can be amplified again. Montaigne wrote: (Essays II vi) "And one might therefore say of me that in this book I have only made up a bunch of other people's flowers, and that of my own I have only provided the string that ties them together". That is very much the author's feeling.

Supplementary reading list

The interested reader will find the References (below) cover the development of manpower planning up to the 1980's. The following texts update the list.

BENNISON M and CASSON J, *Manpower Planning Handbook* (MS), McGraw-Hill, 1984

Incomes Data Services, *Flexibility at Work*, Report No. 360, April 1986

PEACH L, Flexibility: The Flavour of the Future, *Personnel Management*, October 1985

ATKINSON J, Flexibility: Planning for an Uncertain Future, *Manpower Policy & Practice*, Spring 1985 (similar material is available in IMS Report No. 89)

EVANS P (Insead), New Directions in Career Management, *Personnel Management*, December 1986

CRE, Employment Report, March 1987 (for information on equal opportunities and work)

RICHARDS-CARPENTER C, The future of the computerised personnel information system, *Personnel Management*, May 1987

7th National Conference Report on Computers in Personnel IPM/CIP/IMS, July 1988

MALLOCK H, Manpower Modelling with Computer Spreadsheets, *Personnel Management*, May 1986

COWAN N, Change and the Personnel Profession, *Personnel Management*, January 1988

POLLERT A, *The Flexible Firm — a model in search of reality*, IRRU, University of Warwick 1988

IVE T, *Personnel Computer Systems*, McGraw Hill, 1982

BURNS-WINDSOR D, *Developing a Computerised Personnel System*, Brameur/IPM/IMS, 1985

FYFE J, Putting the People back into Manpower Planning Equations, *Personnel Management*, October 1986 (it has been said in Manpower circles for nearly 20 years, but a timely reminder of the importance of people — and not numbers — in planning does not come amiss)

In addition, the Institute of Manpower Studies/Gower *Manpower Policy and Practice* magazine provides a regular source of up-to-date material and practice. The IMS also offers a regular and trustworthy supply of advice and material. The interested reader/manager could do far worse than speak to them.

References and further reading

Books, booklets and articles mentioned in this list have been selected both as references to the main text and to provide a basis for the manager who wishes to study the subject further.

This selection is largely subjective and the exclusion of a publication should not be taken to reflect adversely on its quality.

1   HMSO, *Company Manpower Planning*, 1974. Slightly revised reprint. Widely acclaimed inexpensive booklet
2   STAINER G, *Manpower Planning*, Heinemann, 1971. One of the first substantial books on the subject by a single author. Some well regarded chapters though much of the book is concerned with what many will consider management services rather than personnel techniques
3   BELL D J, *Planning Corporate Manpower*, Longman, 1974. Well written with statistics treated gently
4   BARTHOLOMEW D J and MORRIS B R, *Aspects of Manpower Planning*, EUP, 1971. Based on a selection of good papers presented to the Manpower Planning Study Group during 1968 and 1969 (now the Manpower Society)
5   EDINBURGH GROUP, *Perspectives in Manpower Planning*, IPM, 1967. Ahead of its time though perhaps beginning to date. Still worth reading
6   BARTHOLOMEW D J and SMITH A R, *Manpower and Management Science*, EUP, 1971. A collection of papers from a conference of the Institute of Management Science. A substantial book, probably for the specialist
7a HMSO, *Some statistical techniques of manpower planning*, edited by SMITH A R. CAS occasional paper no 15. This booklet can be understood by the non-specialist and is a good introduction
7b HMSO, *Manpower Planning in the Civil Service*, edited by SMITH A R, 1976. A collection of Civil Service experiences, which is well worth reading

207

8   BARTHOLOMEW D J, *Stochastic Models for Social Processes*, Wiley, 1973 (this is the second edition; the first, published in 1967, did not include manpower planning material). This is one for the specialist though the personnel manager can derive benefit from the narrative

9a   CLOUGH D J et al, *Manpower Planning Models*, EUP, 1974
  b WILSON N A B ed, *Manpower Research*, EUP, 1969
  c SMITH A R ed, *Models of Manpower Systems*, EUP, 1970
  d JESSOP W N ed, *Manpower Planning*, EUP, 1966. This is a series of books which are collections of papers drawn from NATO manpower conferences. Many of the papers are of mathematical nature, though again the narrative includes many useful insights

10   BOWEY A M, *A Guide to Manpower Planning*, Macmillan, 1974. This title would mislead many readers as the book is not as comprehensive as it sounds. It is good on wastage and stability, which is probably Angela Bowey's real field of interest

11   RIVETT P, *Principles of Model Building*, Wiley, 1972. More for the mathematician, but personnel and line managers will probably derive benefit from reading chapter 1

12   LYNCH J J, *Making Manpower Effective*, Part I, Pan 1968
      LYNCH J J, *Making Manpower Effective*, Part II, Pan 1971

13   LAWRENCE J R ed, *Company Manpower Planning in Perspective*, IPM, 1975. Information report proceedings of an IPM/IMS conference held in 1974

14   LASLETT R E, *A Survey of Mathematical Methods of Estimating the Supply of and Demand for Manpower*, Engineering Industry Training Board Occasional Paper, No 1, 1972

IMS conference papers and booklets

15   MORRIS B R, *Recruitment, Promotion and Career Management: the use of quantitative models*, Institute of Manpower Studies, September 1973
16   BRYANT D T, *A Managers Guide to Withdrawal from Work*, IMS, January 1975
17   PURKISS C J, *Introducing Successful Manpower Planning: problems of implementation and information*, IMS, March 1972
18   BENNISON M, *Management Succession: the use of computer based models*, IMS, 1975
19   PURKISS C J, *Identifying Manpower Requirements*, IMS 1971, 1972 and 1975 GN31 & GN77 & 79

Articles

20   BRYANT D T, A Survey of the Development of Manpower Planning Policies, *British Journal of Industrial Relations*, Vol 3, No 3, 1965
21   BARTHOLOMEW D J and FORBES A F, articles on manpower planning, *The Statistician*, Vol 20, No 1, March 1971
22   SMITH A R, Developments in Manpower Planning, *Personnel Review*, Autumn 1971
23   *Personnel Review*, Vol 1, No 3, 1972
24   *Personnel Review*, Vol 2, No 3, 1973
25   BOSWORTH D and EVANS G, Manpower Forecasting — a user's guide, *Personnel Review*, Vol 2, No 4, Autumn 1973. A fairly technical paper
26   BRAMHAM J T, A Study of Staff Succession, *Personnel Review*, Vol 3 No 1, 1974

27 RICE A K, HILL J M and TRIST E L, The Representation of Labour Turnover as a Social Process, *Journal of Human Relations*, No 3, 1950

28 DUNCAN D C, A New Method of Recording Labour Losses, *The Manger*, January 1955

29 BOWEY A M, Labour Stability Curves and a Labour Stability Index, *Brtish Journal of Industrial Relations*, Vol II, No 1 March 1969

30 SILCOCK H, The Phenomenon of Labour Turnover, *Journal of Royal Statistical Society*, A117, 1954

31 LANE K F and Andrew, A method of Labour Turnover Analysis, *Journal of Royal Statistical Society*, A118, 1955

32 HYMAN R, Economic Motivation and Labour Stability, *British Journal of Industrial Relations*, Vol 8, 1970

33 WILD R, Manpower Planning and Job Satisfaction, *Management Decision*, Spring 1973

34 MORRIS B R, Appreciation of Manpower Planning, *O and M Bulletin*, Vol 25, Part 3, 1970

35 Department of Employment *Gazette*. Issues of October 1973, April 1974 and March 1975 include articles on manpower planning, information and unemployment

36 BRAMHAM J T and CLOUGH C M I, *Wastage Analysis*, paper presented to North East Group of the Manpower Society, December 1971

37 *Improving Manpower Information*, Manpower Society Report No 1, July 1974. A report on national manpower information by a working party of the Department of Employment and the Manpower Society

38 CANNON J A, *Human Resource Accounting — a critical comment*, Manpower Society Report No 2, July 1974, (Other articles cover a variety of manpower subjects)

39 *Measuring Labour Productivity*, International Labour Organization, Studies and Reports 75, 1969

40 BRAMHAM J T, A Closer Look at Craft Apprenticeships, *Personnel Management*, March 1974

41 SPRINGHALL J, *Personnel Records and the Computer*, IPM/Industrial Society, 1971

42 The United Kingdom in 1980, Hudson Institute, London Associated Business Programmes, 1974

43 Manpower Society Report No 4, *Manpower in Personnel Management — a suitable case for treatment*, proceedings of a seminar at the IPM Conference, Harrogate 1975 by J T Bramham, J A Cannon, R J Howard, N M Johnston (also published in reference No 45,) 1977

44 *Towards a Comprehensive Manpower Policy*, Manpower Services Commission, 1976

45 *Manpower Planning Papers*, March 1977 Vols 1 and 2 *British Gas, Personnel Division*. A very useful collection of well-known papers on manpower subjects, available from British Gas, 59 Bryanston Street, London W1A 2AZ

46 PURKISS C J, *Manpower Planning Literature*, Department of Employment Gazette, July and November 1976. A wide survey and comment of all literature — well worth looking at for guidance

47 GIBSON H, *Rules of Thumb for Manpower Decisions*, Manpower Society Report No 3, May 1977

48 Manpower Information; Incomes Data Services 1977

49 SMITH A R ed, *Corporate Manpower Planning*, Gower Press, 1980
50 BARTHOLOMEW D J ed, *Manpower Planning*, Penguin 1976
51 THAKUR M, *Manpower Planning*, IPM, 1975
52 PETTMAN B O and TAVERNIER G, *Manpower Planning Workbook*, Gower, 1976
53 JUDKINS P E, DAWSON J A *et al*, *Local Government Manpower Planning: Theory and Practice*, Plenum, 1977
54 Manpower Society (Report No 6), *Manpower Planning: current position and future trends*, 1977
55 Manpower Society (Report No 5), *Manpower Problems in the Current Economic Situation*
56 HUNTER L C, *Labour Shortages and Manpower Policy*. HMSO, 1978. (Manpower Studies, No. 19782)
57 BENNISON M and MORGAN R, *Management of Career Structures*. IMS, 1981
58 WALSH K *et al*, *The UK Labour Market*, IMS, Kogan Page, 1981
59 BENNISON M, *Manpower perspective-employment at the organizational level:* Manpower Society Newsletter, December 1981
60 BRAMHAM *et al*, *Proceedings of the Asian Pacific Conference on Human Resource Management*. Surfers Paradise, Queensland, Institute of Personnel Management (Australia), 1979
61 DRUCKER P F, *The Practice of Management*, Heinemann, 1955
62 CASSON R J, *Re-evaluating Company Manpower Planning in the Light of Some Practical Experiences*, 1977, (also contained in reference 68)
63 BRYANT D and NIEHANS R eds, *Manpower Planning and Organisation Design*, Plenum, 1978
64 *Manpower Planning at Work*, IMS, 1976
65 EVANS A, *A Guide to Manpower Information*, IPM, 1980
66 BILSLAND, Isabel, comp. *Computerizing Personnel Systems: How to choose and where to go.* IPM, 1982
67 WILLE E and HAMMOND V, *The Computer in Personnel Work.* IPM, 1981

Other reading matter

The following is a selection of journals that regularly cover the manpower planning area:
Personnel Review — quarterly
Department of Employment *Gazette* — monthly
Manpower Society Newsletter — monthly
International Labour Office Yearbook, OECD — annual
Social Trends HMSO, — annual
Statistics of Education, HMSO — annual
Department of Employment Manpower Papers, HMSO — *ad hoc*

Index

*Acknowledgement is due to Sony and their advertising agents
for permission to reproduce the Sony car.